I BELIEVE

I BELIEVE

A Journey of Faith and Coping

BY

ED HAZELWOOD

ISBN 978-0-615-59276-3

Copyright September 2010

Ed Hazelwood
Dax Consulting, LLC

AUTHOR'S NOTE

This book was written as a defining statement of how my faith and beliefs were developed, how they have changed, and how they have grown deeper over time, based on life experiences and challenges.

I share many difficult or stressful situations that I have experienced; however, it is written in the spirit of learning from each experience, gaining insight, and being inspired in your own life. I wish you well in your journey!

I was inspired to write this book in a dream on the night of September 4th, 2010.

ACKNOWLEDGEMENTS

I would like to dedicate this book to my wonderful wife, Sue, my caring and compassionate children, James and Julie, and our loyal dog, Dax. By providing me with their love, support and input, I thank them for making this book possible. We thank God for the six wonderful and loving grandchildren we have. They are caring, wonderful children and bring us much joy and happiness. I hope they read this book at some point and find comfort and direction. For my grandchildren: Zander, Skylar, Ayden, Delaney, Carson, and Kennedy.

Additional thanks to Randy Toennies and Stacy Schuett. Randy did the cover art; it is a hand drawn image of a tree by the corner of our home. I have always seen the tree as a symbol of hope and faith of things to come being bare in the winter yet covered with leaves and colorful buds in the spring. Thanks to Stacy for her time, insights and suggestions as editor taking the words I had written and compiling them into a completed book.

I am extremely appreciative of all those that encouraged me during the making of this book.

CHAPTERS

1.	What do you believe?	11
2.	How do you define what you believe?	25
3.	Learning from Life Lessons and Experiences	31
4.	Adventures in Egypt	37
5.	A Wonderful Second Marriage	61
6.	September 11, 2001	71
7.	Major Back Problems	79
8.	Learning from a Heart Attack	85
9.	Learning from Cancer	91
10.	Sports and Life	101
11.	Moving On	133
12.	Developing your Core Support	141
13.	The Toolbox	147
14.	Be an Advocate	169
15.	Your Mission	177
16.	What does it all mean?	185

Chapter One

What do you believe?

Have you ever wondered about your life's journey; how you have arrived at this point in your life with the ideas, dreams, thoughts and beliefs that you currently hold close and believe in? Those parts from your life and experiences have contributed a great deal to who you are today.

Day by day and step by step, you took in, filtered and stored a vast amount of information and experiences: from your family, friends, school, work and the constant barrage of information (and in some cases misinformation) from our 24/7 media. Stop to think about how much of that information you really thought about, analyzed and questioned before storing it in your memory and accepting it as truth.

Might you wonder if all that input of information is based on facts, and the best of your experiences and influences you have had, or have you allowed your environment, friends, and media to shape you. Do you still feel comfortable with who you are, or is it time to take a closer look and update some of those previously accepted principles and ideas.

Basic inputs, thoughts and feelings are guiding you each and every day. Do you know where you are going and why? To clarify, look at the words Lewis Carroll wrote in his famous book, <u>Alice in Wonderland</u>. (Alice came to the crossroads and met the Cheshire cat)
Alice: Would you tell me, please, which way I ought to go from here?
The Cat: That depends a good deal on where you want to get to.
Alice: I don't much care where.
The Cat: Then it doesn't much matter which way you go.

How many of us are like Alice at that point; not really knowing where we are going, how to get there and why. Perhaps we are guided by our faith, our core and self foundation.

The Bible says this about faith: [1]Now faith is the assurance of things hoped for, the conviction of things not seen. [2]Indeed, by faith our ancestors received approval. [3]By faith we understand that the worlds were prepared by the word of God, so that what is seen was made from things that are not visible (Hebrews 11:1-3).

At this point in my life I have changed many of the ideas, conceptions, opinions, perceptions and the handling of events now occurring in my life. It has been a journey filled with some good and some not so good experiences. In retrospect, I understand that many of those experiences were needed to build my faith, add depth to my character, shape my outlook on life and to create my core strength and beliefs.

I believe in God, my wife, my family, my good friends, my dog and in having a mission in life, or at least a strong sense of purpose. I believe God, or perhaps angels, have guided me in life. I have been following His plan for my life. It is by His nudging I am working my way through and beginning to recognize and accept the work that God has called me to do.

This book is written to share with you the journey I have had that developed and built my core strength and beliefs while truly becoming full of faith in God.

I hope this book provides feelings of both empathy and happiness and gives useful ideas and tools for you to use when dealing with your own personal challenges. But most of all, I want this to book to give you hope and inspiration!

As you read my individual life experiences, place yourself in those locations and situations and see if you relate to the emotions and thoughts I did. Live vicariously through my experiences to see how you would have reacted and how such experiences may have added to or changed your core beliefs and faith. At the end of each chapter, you will find questions to stimulate thoughts, discussion and reflection.

It is my intent to share with you how each one of the experiences impacted me and how it was necessary to adjust in each situation and find the best way to deal with each one; to survive, be strong, be compassionate, remain faithful, and to keep in contact with those close to me during those difficult times in order to come out the other side and continue the journey.

In each case or experience both faith in God and my core foundation supported me. Many emotions and thoughts came into my mind. Those emotions were different in each experience and as I thought about each one I started making a list of associated words. The word list continued to grow with each experience and included words such as God, church, love, respect, family, community, humor, confidence, passion, support and empathy.

In any particular challenge, you may find what worked for you in the past does not work or apply this time. I suggest thinking of the word list as a toolbox of words that you can draw from and consider the application of the word to the situation.

I strongly believe that there are times when we need to scale down the size of our ego, empty some of our self righteousness and make room so we can fill ourselves with the love and faith of God. We must also take individual action and participate in life if we are to lead productive and complete lives. That means to me that we must have faith in God and trust in him and His plan for us, but we must also have a core strength built on our experiences and our individual uniqueness. That is your gut instinct that gives you that foundation and sometimes gives you the direction to make a decision when you find that you cannot explain your decision in a purely logical manner. I certainly remember making some difficult decisions based on that principle; when asked to explain my decision making to others, I would say both sides were equal, or I simply did not have as much information available as I would have liked and that I truly believed the choice I made was the right one.

As my late father said, "God helps them that help themselves"! It may be God, your inner strength or your subconscious calling you for a mission and giving you directions. This will depend on your beliefs and how you define what makes up your gut feeling. My gut feeling starts with my faith in God followed by my experiences and associations with my family and friends. I move forward by accepting the mission, trusting my conviction and taking initiative to move in the direction I am led.

I thank God for the wonderful parents I had. My father and mother were honest, hard working people that truly loved each other and their family. They both grew up on farms in Putnam county in Northeast Missouri. They attended church regularly, consistently kept others in their prayers and always offered a shoulder to lean on when it seemed others needed it. They had strong character and great common sense built by hard work and their love of God. My parents were both very religious and I have great memories of going to church on Sundays, attending prayer meetings on special nights, participating in Bible school and summer religious revivals.

At a young age my father was sent off to battle in World War II. He was trained then shipped out to the front, landing at Utah beach in Normandy. After a few days in active battle, he was severely wounded and spent many months hospitalized. He endured multiple operations before being discharged. He was disabled but he refused to let that stop him from fulfilling any hopes or desires he had for himself and his life. He came back home, got married and spent most of his adult life as a farmer in Missouri. I remember growing up and learning my role on the farm. It was most exciting when my father first taught me to drive the farm tractors and how all the many implements such as a plow, harrow, planter and cultivator and harvesting equipment worked during the planting, growing and harvesting seasons.

We always had a multitude of animals on the farm as well. We had dairy cows and beef cows which were typically Angus. We had hogs and even a couple of horses for awhile. We typically had three or four cats, and always had a dog. I enjoyed being around them and playing with them. I attended numerous elementary schools in the eastern part of Putnam county including Graysville, Martinstown and the one room school in the Sidney area. I graduated from Unionville High school in Unionville, Missouri and was President of my 1963 graduating class. After graduating from school and leaving home home, I fondly remembered the animals and how they fit into life on the farm, and how they were a warm memory of my boyhood years.

My father was a strong, loving father to me and we shared many wonderful moments. I will always remember sitting on his lap when I was only four or five years old and listening to programs and stories on the radio just a few feet from the oil stove. The radio was the entertainment center of the day; a beautiful dark wooden cabinet that held an AM and FM radio and on the bottom shelf a phonograph that would play either 45 or 78 rpm records. There was a second door to the left that provided storage space for the records. This was a much quieter, more private and focused time. We sat together and listened intently; focused on the words of the characters in the story or program. Since this was radio, we had to use our imagination to create the visuals of the story and the events happening. One thing I remember that is different than watching TV as we do today is that we talked more during the program. We shared our impressions of what was happening as we created the story in our minds as we listened to the words. I can still close my eyes and clearly see us sitting together in that chair enjoying the story and each others company. It was the perfect ending to a long day of work.

My father worked hard all his life and did not stop until he reached retirement age. He remained involved in church and served as a deacon for a time. After his retirement from farming, we moved to Wright Cityy just a few miles East of St. Louis. He then guided us with his seasoned advice until his passing in 1995. My father passed away before my mother and this was particularly difficult on me as I was very close to him and knew his passing would leave a void in me.

I was very fortunate to be given the opportunity to be with him for his last hours as he was hospitalized a couple days before his passing. I was with him and my mother for a day or so as we waited and hoped he would pull through one more time, but the second day came and his condition worsened. Each hour was critical. My mother and I went in together to see him at the end of the day, he was having a hard time but was attempting to keep his spirits up. He talked with us and told us everything was fine. He even convinced us to go home, rest, and come back to see him the next day.

When we came back the following day, he wasn't doing well. The doctors said he was struggling enormously and that certain functions and organs were beginning to shut down. He would not be able to see or talk with us at this point but would still be able to hear us. My mother and I went in together for just a minute, then I had a few minutes with him in private to tell him how much he had meant to me, how his love and guidance would be with me forever and how I loved him. I give thanks to God for allowing me the time to speak those last words to my father.

From both my father and from living on a rural farm until I graduated from High School, I learned how to work, appreciate nature, have respect for animals and pets, form a strong belief in God, value a man's word and doing what is right. I had a great respect for him and what he had gone through being born in the tough time of the early 1900's. His teaching and everyday example of being honest, treating others as you wanted to be treated and his guidance gave me what I believe was the very beginning of my core strength foundation and building blocks of faith in dealing with life on an everyday basis. When I thought of all that he had gone through and compared them to the specific issues I was dealing with, my problems didn't seem nearly as significant.

His stance was if that if your troubles could be worse; you could handle them. You can do it!

How this affected me and what I learned–

From my father, I learned to keep my outlook simple and not let things or life get too complicated.

The immediate impact was a huge feeling of loss, an empty place in my inner being. In my conversations with others, I could no longer talk about what he did yesterday, or what he was planning to do tomorrow. I would catch myself thinking that I should call him to see how he was doing, but then I'd remember with a sharp pang of hurt that I could no longer call him. I learned then to bow my head, or to look to the sky and the heavens to talk with my father. I would often say a simple prayer that I knew he was in heaven with God, and that he was with me in thought and spirit. I would thank him for all his love and the advice he had given me.

This was a very difficult time, as my father was my first parent to pass away; this was the reality check that things do change, my parents would not be there forever. I was fortunate to still have my mother around for a time.

When my mother passed away ten years later, the timing was not as favorable. I had moved again and was not able to be there with her in her last hours. I had visited her a few weeks earlier and knew at that time, it would be my last time. My son and daughter left their own families to be with me on that visit. I remember telling them on that day we visited my mother, to pay special attention and respect as this would be the last time we would see her.

A few weeks after our visit, I received a call from the nurse in early evening telling me that my mom was not doing well. I asked a couple of questions, and then I asked the nurse how serious this was and if I should fly out the next morning. I was told there was not enough time and that my mother would not make it through the night. I remember thinking how amazing it was that doctors and modern medicine could do so much to keep us well and in some cases prolong life, and that they could provide treatments and procedures to give us hope. But when it comes to the end, the caretakers that spend time each and every day with our loved ones know us best and can predict with in a few hours when our journey will end. In this case, my mother passed away within a few hours.

My mother was always full of compassion, love, comfort and an eagerness to help others. My mother had grown up in the country and was determined to get a college degree and become a teacher. During those early years when she was attending grade school and high school she often had to walk several miles to school. She went on to college and received her college degree. After graduation, she became a teacher and taught for more than 40 years. When teaching in the rural one room schools, she was faced with walking or riding a horse for transportation. She told me stories of the hardship, particularly during the winter months, walking through the deep snow or riding her horse and yet always being willing to take the time to help others in need.

My mother will always be remembered as being extremely compassionate, giving and having an incredible capacity for supporting and encouraging people. She was always 100%

supportive of me all through school, praising me for my accomplishments and always believing in my abilities to do my very best. She was my teacher for one year, and as most of the schools in our area were one room schools with eight grades in a single room or building, I went to the same school with her for three or four years. She was a master at asking questions and understanding how I or anyone else felt. She never changed and continued to put others before herself until she was no longer able to take care of herself.

My mother's passing was hard on me as was my fathers, but in a different way. Her attitude toward those around her was always extremely positive. She reinforced a strong belief in the individual, always helped one feel good about themselves, always looked for the upside in any situation and she was always looking to move forward.

She always made me feel special. It was hard for me to believe in all those great things she would say to me because I thought of myself as average. She was always telling me I was smart and ambitious. With the constant support and love from my mother, I always wanted to be better, take the initiative to make things happen and to change for the better.

Even though it has been several years now after my parents passing, their spirit is still with me. It's always there in my core being, acting as an internal compass to guide me in those times when I am uncertain.

There are times in all our lives when something unexpected happens when we aren't ready. It is at these times we need to have faith and draw from our reservoir of strength. It may be uncomfortable, extremely difficult, and even painful. However it is as though God has given us trials and trying experiences in order to allow us the opportunity to build and strengthen our faith and fellowship. We are to learn from these hard times so that we grow, increase our core strength and are better prepared for the next trial.

It is during hard times that we have the unique opportunity to really look deep into our minds and our bodies to understand the best we can how we are reacting and how we are feeling. Does this situation compare with any previous experiences or feelings, and do we have the tools to cope? If not, what strengths and weaknesses exist within us? What do we need to do to cope, to resolve this issue and to move forward? What will we have learned about ourselves and what new can we learn from this experience that builds on our faith and our coping skills? I encourage you to look at the toolbox section and think about how this might be applied in your life.

Questions for Reflection

1. What influences have your parents had on the shaping of your core?

2. Who or what experiences have heavily influenced the shaping of your core?

3. Is there a difference between who or what has shaped your core versus who or what *should* have shaped your core?

4. Have both good and bad times shaped your core? Which has had a greater influence and why do you think that is?

Chapter Two

How do you define what you believe?

I always tried very hard to maintain a positive attitude and read every article and book I could get my hands on regarding the power of positive thinking and in being an optimist. One of the books I read early on and have referred to many times since is <u>The Power of Positive Thinking</u> by Dr. Norman Vincent Peale. This is one of the books I have always had on my bookshelf and frequently turn to when looking to find a profound thought or the answer to one of life's challenges. For most of us, it can be exceptionally difficult to set to words what you believe in, the implications of your beliefs, how they influence the way you act, and how they are responsible for creating the person you are on a daily basis.

You may want to begin using a notebook or journal to write your thoughts down. Write key thoughts or beliefs you have and may use to cope and guide you through your daily life with your work, family, friends, faith, sports and hobbies.

Each one of us will certainly find a time when we are unsure of a decision to make or how we make it through the next day or month. It is during those times that most of us need to not only be able to reach into our inner being and core for comfort and direction but to also have family, friends, religious guidance and coworkers that we can trust in and talk to about our burdens and decisions.

I believe we must have faith in a higher power and plan or reason for our life. I was raised in a very religious home where we attended church regularly, as well as the summer revivals, and I attended Bible school. This was the basis for my core strength foundation and then was overlaid with a good home life and a loving mother and father.

As I grew into a teenager, I attended high school and learned different beliefs and opinions. This became a different layer in my core belief and changed some of my earlier opinions and thoughts. During my high school years at Unionville High is when I had instilled lifelong beliefs and strengths that formed my direction and allowed me to know who I was and what I wanted to do.

I believe in a worldwide conspiracy that there are people all over the world just waiting to help us if we just reach out. There are those in life that we seem to gravitate towards, feel comfortable with and trust to be honest when we ask them for an opinion. There are a lot of truly good people in this world that will always do the right thing.

I believe that dogs are our best friends and that they are here to comfort and calm us. I believe lady bugs are good luck. Some take comfort and believe in dreams and gain insight and guidance from their dreams. Others believe in angels and report firsthand experiences with them.

It took me a long time to accept that we need to understand both our body and mind. We have to know our physical body and be able to recognize when it is hurting. Furthermore, we must listen to what it is telling us and learn how to take care of it. Equally important as understanding out physical body, we must understand our mind. It's vital to monitor our conscious and subconscious minds and continue to develop them. We really need to be mindful of our thoughts when thinking about experiences and how the mind can take us down the path of negative thinking. I have read in numerous places the mind can make heaven of hell, and a hell of heaven.

I strongly believe that it is important to monitor your thoughts and realize if your thinking is positive or negative. If it is negative there comes a time when you have to tell yourself to stop that line of negative thinking and set your mind to focus on realistic ideas and positive thoughts. This follows the idea that there is a time when you must let things go!

I believe that there are times when humor is an extremely useful tool to relieve our burden and help get us through the moment or the day. Someone once said to me, "I have to laugh to keep from crying"! In some instances it may be that humor and laughter is the thing we need to break the train of negative thoughts, clear our mind and get back to the present moment.

I believe this goes to the core of your personal beliefs. Those basic true beliefs will support and comfort you when you are backed in a corner, stressed out, feeling alone and adrift, and when you are uncertain about things.

Put yourself in the situation where someone is asking you question after question, drilling down to you basic core beliefs. You need to know who you really are, be able to say it, stand for it and believe it whole heartedly.

Questions for Reflection

1. Do you remember when you first began to understand who you were and the direction you were headed?

2. How did those beliefs and self identity change and develop as you grew older?

3. Was there a defining moment when you changed one of your core beliefs?

4. How did you accept that change?

Chapter Three

Learning from life lessons and experiences

I believe many of the diverse situations and circumstances we encounter on our life journey are meant to provide us with opportunity for growth and shaping. We accomplish this by learning from these events. The learning can come to us through people we meet and interact with, through events we are involved in or observe, and through careful and purposeful listening.

Dreams may also play a very valuable role in our life and offer a tremendous opportunity to reflect on the current events in our life. By dreaming we are able to live through them again, even if only briefly, interpret them and learn from them. Many of us have dreams but do not take the time to recall or think about them. I believe that dreams are important enough that we should make a conscious effort to dream and to recall those dreams each morning to see what they might tell us not only about what has happened but also to provide us with a second opportunity to gain new insights for the future. I believe that only by making a conscious effort the next morning after the dream can we gain an understanding of what might have triggered that dream. Then we are able to reflect back to recent events in order to better understand that what we see and hear everyday impacts our conscious and subconscious mind. I believe from my own experiences that I can tie the dream to events or conversations from the previous day or two.

During the writing of this book, I became much more aware of my dreams. Once I increased my awareness level, I realized that I was dreaming almost every night.

As I talked with others about my experiences they shared with me that they too had dreams, and they looked to their dreams for questions and answers and in some cases guidance from God.

I then started a dream journal that I kept by my bed. I would often have more than one dream per night, so I would write a brief description of what the dream was about when I woke in the middle of the night. I would then write my complete recollection of my dreams upon awakening that morning. Later in the day, or perhaps the next day, I would read over my notes and tie the information together in my mind. I was always looking to connect the dream with events and thoughts from the past to see if the dream might have an answer to an issue I was dealing with.

I would record in detail what the dream was about, who was in it, and where it took place. The next day I would sit down and read what I had written about the previous night's dreams and try to interpret and understand the meaning within the dream.

The following is just a brief example of a dream I had shortly after starting on this book: A forest fire had caused a fire in the home of an old friend I was visiting. By coincidence, three persons that had recently been released from prison were in the area and came right over and helped extinguish the fire. Afterwards in talking with them we discussed why they would help someone they did not know. One of the reasons given was that inside they had no sense of purpose or anything to look forward to as each day was the same, they just knew they needed to help someone else in need and had a feeling of wanting to care for someone. They wanted to do better, overcome adversity and show compassion for others. We talked for quite some time, but I do not have recollection of who they were or what they looked like. I do remember we talked about inner pride and about how to work with and provide guidance and support to those in prison, or recently released.

I believe part of the message to me in the dream was that there are many people that have very little support or guidance in prison, as well as in many other situations of disadvantage. They may not have the family or friends to support them emotionally or financially. They do not have a support system that offers them a sense of hope. There are opportunities for many of us who are able to provide support to those in need. We should be listening for those opportunities and when we hear of them, take action and find a way to be of assistance.

A dream a few months ago was about a really strange event involving taking my car to a big shop. It was a very large compound facility that seemed to be family owned with a very bad reputation. I parked my car and walked inside to talk to someone about a repair. Within a few minutes I walked back out and found that they had taken my car someplace else, replaced it with an old dilapidated vehicle and then proceeded to try and tell me that it was mine!

Things went from bad to worse. I walked back inside the gated fence and back into the building to talk with someone that could correct this situation. They said the only way I could leave was if I did everything they wanted me to and part of that was to pay a very high price to get a better car with no option of getting mine back. From there it was like being in prison. I was in their office inside a compound like facility so I did not argue. We were talking some, but there were multiple people on their side so I was thinking what to say next. Then they brought my wife in and she was being held as well. I was terrified of what the outcome might be and knew that I had to resist. I started toward her, grasped her hand and slowly we started moving away from the workers and toward an open door. Even though we only moved a few feet, we realized they were not stopping us. I then asked God for help, told him I loved him and that we would follow him. Things got better very fast; it was like we were both floating a few feet off the ground and moving away from the captors. With my wife at my side, I told her how much I loved her. We both said out loud that we were putting our faith in God and pledging our love and faith to him. All the workers that had us captive initially had followed us a short distance but were rapidly dropping back. Only one of them was staying within a short distance and appeared to be walking while we were floating above the ground. The more we prayed to God and confirmed our faith in him, the faster we moved away from the captors until we were out the gate and free.

Even though this was a dream, we understood this to mean that you cannot just go along with something you don't believe in. If you do, you will be led in any direction by whoever is leading you. This may be the devil or any other temptation. Once you take the initiative and trust that God is with you, you have all the power and direction you need.

The Bible tells us in Philippians 4:13: "I can do all things through Him who strengthens me." Depending on the particular Bible you are reading the verse may read slightly different: "I have the strength to face all conditions by the power that Christ gives me." I have the first version of this verse in a large frame in my office so that I see it every day.

Questions for Reflection

1. Leave a pad of paper by your bedside tonight. If you wake up during the night, jot down a few brief notes about the dream you had. Fill in the details upon awakening in the morning and reflect on the possible meaning. Was there a message or lesson to be learned in your dream? What can you take away from it?

2. How might these messages change or develop your faith and core strength?

3. Where do you get this strength to challenge what lies in front of you and take action or go forth as God tells us in multiple ways?

4. What Bible verses or other quotes come to mind about when thinking about facing your challenges?

Chapter Four

Adventures in Egypt

Several years prior to the life experiences I had with a heart attack and cancer, I had a major work related event that tested my core beliefs and strength which eventually ended in greatly reinforcing and adding to my core strength. I was offered a two year assignment as a communications technology consultant in Cairo, Egypt.

The decision to go or not to go was one of the most difficult decisions I have been called to make. It was the root of many heated discussions with friends and family.
I immediately knew that I really wanted to go on this assignment, but there were too many other factors holding me back from committing. I was recently divorced and my son and daughter were only of the ages nine and six. This would mean long periods of separation for both them and me. My mind was telling me not to go, that this was impossible, that I would not see my kids, that my parents would not want me to go, and that I was not even certain I could make the adjustments and fulfill a two year assignment.

I did not sleep much for a couple of nights, but knew that I still wanted to go. If I could just take my kids to Egypt with me during the summer months when they were out of school, I definitely wanted to go. I discussed this idea with the company and they said yes. They wanted me on the project and arrangements would be made for my son and daughter to join me for two summers. This became one of the most rewarding decisions I have ever made and resulted in unbelievable experiences for my son, daughter and myself. This was my calling; we were going to Egypt!

It was an adventure from the very beginning. We were traveling from the Midwest to Egypt knowing no one except for one family we briefly met that had young children. They said they would spend time with us during the summer.

When we left for Egypt we still knew very little about what the initial accommodations would be like until I found a flat to rent. We were told that a guide would meet us at the airport in Cairo and would take us to the hotel where we would stay for a few weeks. Finally the big day arrived, and the three of us boarded the plane in St. Louis and flew to Europe, then we changed planes a couple of more times before arriving in Egypt.

We made the connection with our guide and soon our luggage was loaded into a small car for the drive to the hotel. During our drive, we were intrigued and in awe of how different the city was. As the drive continued on longer than expected, I began asking the driver how far it was to our hotel since I had assumed we would be staying in a hotel close to the airport. He just replied that it was quite a ways further. I then asked what the hotel was like since I really had no idea what the accommodations might be. He said that it would be a nice hotel. I then proceeded to ask what the name was in hopes it might be a major chain I would be familiar with. He said it was The Holiday. I had not heard of that and began having some concerns because my kids were with me.

After what seemed to be a very long time, we saw three large pyramids in the distance and remarked to the driver how big and very impressive they were. He said they are just across the road from our hotel. Soon we saw a very nice hotel just ahead and in a couple of minutes we pulled up in front of a huge, new Holiday Inn! It was striking and the view of the pyramids from there was spectacular.

The summer was filled with many new adventures for the three of us, and even the few weeks we were at the hotel were wonderful. My son and daughter swam in the pool everyday, we went up to the pyramids often, visited the Sphinx and even rode camels a couple times.

It was a tremendous learning experience for them as the surroundings, the people, the language and the customs were so very different than the Midwest in the good old USA. It was so good to see my son and daughter at that young age make friends with the children from the company group I was working with and also with kids that were living or visiting there with their parents from other countries such as France, England and other middle eastern countries. One day when we were still at the hotel, I remember sitting at a large table in the pool and lobby area watching my son and daughter playing a card game with two children and their father. We were there for an hour or so, and we had a great time just watching, smiling and laughing. The greatest part of this is the fact that we did not speak any Arabic and they did not speak a word of English! We had a great time communicating without any words.

The other really amazing place we visited a few times, generally on a day off, was the world famous Bazaar in Cairo known as Khan Al Kahlili. This was one of the most interesting and fun places to go. This huge, very crowded market offers almost every conceivable item of wood, silver, brass, gold, and cloth in the style and décor of the country of Egypt including gold and silver cartouches.

It was a real treat to go down to the market place and just wander through a part of this vast area, through the narrow walk ways and stopping at the small shops to talk with the craftsman, enjoy a cup of tea and bargain for goods. It was an art. The prices were always too high, and the fun started when you said no, not interested. Then the price would come down. To get the best price, you would have to turn away at least two or three times as if to leave. The merchants were nice, and you always had to have a cup of tea with them during this process. After a few trips to the market, I was hooked. I became a regular visitor during the two years there. Many times I would just go to visit some of the shops and talk. I would tell them up front this was just a visit and we had wonderful conversations.

At the end of the summer, my son and daughter left to go back to the United States to their mother. That was a sad day, but we all had many wonderful memories of spending the summer together in an amazing, interesting country that we never would have dreamed of having the chance to visit. By the time they went back home, I had moved into a flat in downtown Cairo and began exploring the city and some of the exciting adventures it offered. To share all those adventures would be a book in itself; however, I hope you enjoy the following three I have provided.

I-Climbing the Great Pyramid

There were many pyramids in Egypt, and I was fortunate enough to climb up a couple of the smaller ones. I spent a lot of time visiting several sites. The ones that fascinated me the most were the three large ones at Giza, the ones most visible in the Cairo area and the ones made famous by being located by the Sphinx. The three pyramids had originally been constructed quite a distance from the main part of the city of Cairo, but over the years the city had steadily been growing out toward the Giza pyramids and the Sphinx, so by the time I arrived they were at the edge of the city.

For me this was a fascinating area. The pyramids were remarkable; three were together and the Great Pyramid being so large and so well preserved. The base of the Great Pyramid covered some 13 acres and it was as tall as a 50 story building. It became a favorite place for me to go in the evenings for a place to sit, think, reflect on where I was and the events that were shaping my life each and every day. For me this was the most ideal place to relax, meditate and collect my thoughts from the day. Climbing some 50 to 75 feet up the corner gave me a vantage point with a gentle breeze blowing in my face and having a stunning view of the huge city of Cairo with its millions of sparkling lights. Then turning my head to look behind me, the shear black darkness of the desert was such a calm and peaceful feeling.

During that time, I was sharing my experiences with other friends there, and a couple of us got together and began riding horses that we rented from stables in the area. From there we would ride through the orange groves just a short distance away. We would ride late in the afternoon or early in the evening, often staying out until after dark. It was comforting yet invigorating riding from the orange groves. We started by a small river in the flat area and continued on past the pyramids. It was during those rides that I really learned how to ride the Arabian horses with a Western saddle as well as the English saddle.

Early one clear and cool morning, three of us met at the base of the Great Pyramid just up the hill from the Sphinx. We had a guide with us and we were determined to climb to the very top of the Great Pyramid reaching some 500 feet. We were looking forward to making this climb, seeing a view we had only heard about and of course being able to go back and tell everyone that we had successfully made the climb. This feat was something we had talked about several times, but our friends always talked us out of it due to the dangers in climbing and the stories heard of others attempts that had resulted in fatal falls and ultimately death. The angle of the climb was steep, the individual stone blocks were some 3 feet high, and we used no ropes or safety equipment to harness ourselves. One slip and fall almost certainly resulted in a domino effect, falling all the way to the bottom.

I was second in line as we began the climb. We moved slowly, placing our feet carefully. We aimed for a firm handhold on the edge of the block above us, pulling ourselves up enough to reach for the next block. We climbed for some time not saying much, and then the lead climber stopped and said to turn and look out into the sky. I looked over my right shoulder in the direction of Cairo, but before taking in the view, I saw how high we were and how little stone we were clinging to. My stomach dropped. I managed to hold on and kept my focus by not looking down. I just stared, spellbound by the magnificent view of the city of Cairo.

After regaining our confidence, we continued upwards and did not stop but once or twice more before reaching the top. The very top of the pyramid was flat, only about the size of a small room that had been formed by rocks tumbling off. We stood on top and stared into the distance, turning in each direction to take in the breathtaking view. The pyramid was at the highest point in this area and was by far, taller than anything else around. There was a slight breeze blowing and as we gazed into the distance, we burned this image into our memories making it last forever.

We stayed for an hour more just talking and taking in the view, knowing how very fortunate we were for having been given the opportunity. We were a handful of selected people that traveled to Egypt, made it to this point and then actually climbed to the top of the Great Pyramid in Cairo!

When it was time to go down the pyramid, I asked the guide how we were going to do this. He said we would do it the same way we got up, one step at a time. As I walked closer to the edge and looked some 500 feet down at the narrow ledges and the repetitive three foot drops that were considered to be our steps, I asked again; how is it possible to walk down when we don't have anything to hold on to? He said that bending over to hold on to a stone with your hands was not something you wanted to do or it would cause you to slip and fall. The blocks are so high and the pyramid is so steep that one slip is enough to send you to the very bottom.

With that we got our heads together and decided we had no choice but to start the decent, focus on our own efforts and take it step by step. We spread out a few feet from each other and literally stepped straight off the edge to the few inches of edge sticking out two to three feet below us. Our adrenaline pushed us to continue descending in this chilling manner until we reached the bottom. What a journey; it was the most exciting yet terrifying thing I have ever done.

II- Saddle or No Saddle: Falling off the Horse.

On a weekend afternoon, I decided to take a slow and relaxing ride on a horse from one of the stables in the Giza area. I started by riding around the three pyramids then continued on down by the Sphinx. Due to the large number of tourists in the area during that time of the day, I had to ride the horse on the paved road rather than on the sand pathway in order to make more room for everyone to walk.

As I made my way down the middle of the road, I was looking ahead to see how soon we might be past everyone so we could get back on the sand. I could tell my horse was not comfortable walking on the asphalt surface. Then it happened; my horse slipped and fell down on the road. I immediately attempted to get off so he could get back up. However, he was already starting to get back on his feet, and I had not yet cleared the saddle as he was jumping up. The next thing I knew, he was up on all four feet and I was being tossed off to the side.

As he began to run, I realized that I still had one boot caught in the stirrup and was now being dragged along with my back against the asphalt. As he continued running, I raised my head and pulled my shoulders forward, rounding them so I was sliding just on my back. Thankfully the road was smooth and I had on a light denim jacket so I wasn't in much pain as I slid down the road. I turned from side to side hoping I could break loose. I noticed several tourists walking along both sides of the road yelling and pointing at me. A couple of them were raising their cameras to take a picture. I wonder if anyone has a good shot of that (please contact me if you do).

After that episode, I changed from a Western saddle to an English saddle, as they were smaller and seemed to be easier to get in and out of. After many more hours of riding, I gave up saddles entirely and from then on only rode bareback.

I soon discovered that being an experienced rider did not entirely eliminate problems between myself and my four footed friends. One evening, a friend and I rode out into the dessert after dark to a small restaurant for dinner and a drink. After dinner, I came out and quickly jumped up on my horse's back surprising him and causing him to throw his head back just as I was landing on top of him. Due to his abrupt movement and throwing his head back with a jerking motion, I was being pitched forward. As a result, his head hit me square on the chin, and the next thing I knew I was flat on my back in the sand. A quick lesson learned.

III- The President's Assassination

The 6th of October was a very important day in Egypt. It was a day of remembrance, pride, celebration and high emotions for the thousands in attendance of the celebration. President Muhammad Anwar Sadat would be there attending the eighth anniversary of the Yom Kippur war with Israel as Field Marshal of the armed forces.

I had been in the country a full year now and felt a real connection to the country and its people. It was an exceptionally emotional event that consisted of a large parade that called for tight security. As Americans working in the county, we had been advised not to attend such events and it was best to not get involved.

Since I had been in the county for more than a year, met many people and truly enjoyed working there, I wanted to attend. Of course, being impressed watching the practice for the parade by big military trucks, tanks, and people, I thought it would be a great experience to be there and watch. Not only did I want to see the airplanes flying overhead, but the chance to see the country's leaders including President Anwar Sadat was something too good to pass up!

I had a wonderful young fellow from Egypt as my driver at the time, and I discussed the situation with him. He was very excited that I wanted to attend and said he would be happy to go with me. He cautioned me on what I already knew; the crowd would be huge and everyone would be very emotional.

As we made our way that fateful day of October 6th, 1981, masses of people and countless cars moved slowly around us as we neared the parade grounds. My driver was doing his best to avoid the largest part of traffic and was searching for a possible place to park. Finally after an hour or so, a parking space was found and we began walking alongside crowds of others toward the review stands where we knew President Sadat and other high ranking government officials would be. The closer we could get to that area, the better view we would have. However, we knew security would be tight and we would need some luck to get a good viewing spot for the parade.

We soon came to a checkpoint formed by a solid ring of Egyptian military and police officers, all with some very serious looking weapons. We talked with a couple of them briefly and explained we just wanted to see the equipment in the parade. They let us through and we continued our walk toward the review stands which was still some distance away. After a few minutes we came to a second ring of security. This time it was more difficult to get through and we noticed that no one seemed to get past this point. Finally I found one officer that spoke English and I showed him my American passport. I told him I was living and working in the county and would really like to see the parade. He eventually let me through, but not my driver. We agreed to meet back at the car after the parade and parted.

I then walked past several people until I was right at the end of the review stands about 80 to 100 feet from the middle where President Sadat would be sitting. When realizing this was as close as I could get, I was satisfied with my viewpoint.

The very first part of the parade was already in front of the review stand and as I looked to my left I actually saw President Sadat and his entourage. After watching the parade just a few minutes, an Egyptian official came directly to me and asked a question in Arabic that I did not understand. I told him I was American and did not understand his question. Then in perfect English, he asked me who I was and what I was doing there. I explained to him that I was living and working in Egypt and wanted to see the parade I had missed last year. He then asked for identification and I handed him my passport. He opened it, took a quick look, and then put it in his pocket. He told me not to move from where I was and he would be back. I did not object seeing that he was very courteous and was carrying an automatic weapon. I am not certain what his position was and he was not in uniform, but this didn't worry me. I thought he would simply verify my identity and return my passport well before the parade ended.

I stayed where I was and enjoyed watching the soldiers march past, the trucks and specialty vehicles carrying various types of missiles and guns drive past and of course the very large tanks roll by. Some of them were rotating the gun from side to side. The ground shook as they drove past and the noise was surprisingly loud.

I continued to enjoy the parade and was also checking once in a while to make sure the security official that had taken my passport was still in sight. I saw him from time to time, but he never came back to me as he walked a section of the review stands. I remember seeing a large number of what I assumed were all security personnel walking both sides of the street, as well as several people on horseback.

I thought it might have been nearing the end of the parade. There were soldiers marching past and a flat bed type military vehicle rolling by with just a few soldiers standing in the back. President Sadat stood fully erect and was saluting the soldiers in front of him. At the same time, a group of French fighter jets came over us from behind. They were in close formation and very low. The roar was incredible! All eyes were on the fighter jets as they went over us, and then they performed a big upward loop twisting over and turning to come back above the parade area.

As the noise from the planes faded but our eyes were still focused up in the sky, I became aware of strange sounds on the ground to my left. As I shifted my eyes back to the parade route I realized the sounds were a popping noise. I heard pop, pop, pop, pop in rapid succession. Then I focused on the center of the stands and saw President Sadat surrounded by Vice President Mubarak and others. Some of the soldiers in the parade stopped. Their guns were pointed directly at the President and the popping noise continued. As I watched in disbelief, the popping continued and I knew the President had been shot, probably multiple times.

Then I realized that the security personal was shouting at the crowd to run back and get away. Other security personnel had their weapons raised and were running towards the shooters. People were crying, horses were running, spectators were screaming, and I realized I could be in great danger from the vast number of people running in panic.

I took one quick look around for the guy with my passport and saw him running toward the shooters. I decided to leave my passport with him and turned to run. My thoughts at that time were on the tragedy of what had just happened, if I would be able to get out of there without being hurt, and if my driver would be at the car.

It took several minutes for me to walk through the mass of hysterical people, but I finally reached my car and my driver was there. As we drove from the area, we talked about what had happened and what the event would mean for the country of Egypt. My driver was very upset and just kept repeating that this was very, very bad. He drove to the area where he lived and I took the car from there so he could be with his family. As I slowly drove away, I looked back to see my driver hurrying, half walking, half running to get to his family and warn them of what we had just witnessed.

As I drove carefully through the city traffic to get to my midtown living quarters, I realized that most of the population probably had not heard of the horrifying event yet. As soon as I was back in my flat downtown, I turned the radio on and checked both VOA (Voice of America) and BBC (British Broadcasting Corporation). There was no mention of any incident at the October 6th Parade!

I then called a couple of my American co-workers to check with them. When I described the events that I saw, they were in disbelief. They said they had not heard of anything and if something happened then the President must be okay, otherwise there certainly would have been news on the radio and TV.

I assured them that I was there and unbelievably close to the action. I told them that based on the scene I witnessed and the number of shots I heard, not only was President Sadat shot, but he must be dead and the government wanted to keep it quiet until they had control of the city. My co-workers, still in disbelief, said that it probably would be wise to stay in and not go out in the city until we knew the situation. It certainly could be a rebellion and the local citizens would surely be emotional.

I stayed in my flat reading and listening to the radio for any news at all. It was about mid day so I pulled the window drapes so no one could see in and I could pace and walk around in private.

Finally, in the early evening, some six or eight hours after the actual shooting, there was a brief announcement on the radio that there had been a shooting incident at the Parade and that President Sadat had died. Later there was word of some 'shooting in the streets' in the area I resided as well as a couple of other areas.

The next day we did not go to work and instead listened to the news and talked with each other by telephone. I was concerned about where this might go and if all of us would be in danger. What if we needed to leave the country and I didn't have my passport.

Later in the second day I heard that the government, under Vice President Mubarak, had ordered that tanks be located at the radio and television stations as well as at key bridges and major roads. After a couple of days we met at the office to share information and to get direction from our company management.

Our project offices were in a government building and it was now surrounded by some 75 to 100 armed soldiers. They encircled the building and were standing so close they could almost touch each other.

Our management told us to stay close to the office or our flats and minimize our exposure in the city. They would be in constant touch with our local Egyptian government contacts for frequent updates on the situation. They were also in touch with our U.S. Company office and were keeping our families updated on our situation.

The next morning the radio, television and news media reported that 'President Sadat of Egypt has died after being shot by gunmen who opened fire as he watched an aerial display at a military parade. A number of other dignitaries including foreign diplomats were killed or seriously wounded. The Egyptian authorities have declared a state of emergency.'

I had to tell our project management that I was right up front at the parade and that a government security person had taken my passport. They reported that to the American Embassy in Cairo and were told two things: initially, I should not have been at the parade as it was a highly charged event and anything could happen, and secondly, chances were not good that I would ever see my passport again as American passports were worth a lot of money on the black market.

As is turned out, God was with me. A few days after the event, an Egyptian military officer walked into the American Embassy in downtown Cairo and returned my passport! What a relief. I knew I could leave now.

At the end of my two year assignment, I reflected on my time and knew that even with all things considered, I had gained knowledge and my life was richer from this experience. I wanted to continue with this lifestyle and started thinking about a possible new international assignment.

I began talking with others in the international community about possible opportunities. I found that at this particular time the good assignments were very limited. I also knew that I would not consider a long term assignment in a country that was not absolutely safe to take my son and daughter.

As it turned out, there were no such assignments available for me. I ended my time in Egypt and came back to the U. S. to a temporary assignment in Washington, DC, working at the

Dulles Airport on a special project for my company but still as a member of their International Division.

After working as a part of this team for several months, there was a short term opportunity in Beirut, Lebanon, after the flare up between a fraction group and Israel. It had resulted in Israeli forces moving into the Beirut area and due to the ensuing fighting, caused much damage to the communications infrastructure.

I received a call from our International headquarters office asking me if I would be interested in a short term international assignment in Beirut to help assess the extent of the damage to the communications infrastructure and putting together a plan to reestablish working communications. I was very interested in this opportunity and said I would. They said they would call the organization I was currently working with to get everything cleared and a schedule established. I would probably need to leave in two to four weeks and fly into Europe to be met by a military officer who would accompany me to Beirut.

My excitement did not last very long for this trip; I was told a couple of days later that my role was vital on the current project and I could not be pulled out at a moment's notice for an unknown period of time. As it turned out, that was the end of my international assignments. I moved to Atlanta a few months later and accepted a permanent position on the domestic project.

How this affected me and what I learned-

This two year assignment involved more mental struggles and emotional stress than I ever could have imagined, but in the end it provided many benefits and fond memories. I spent invaluable time with my son and daughter when they traveled and lived with me for two years. We shared many incredible adventures: we went to the pyramids, the Sphinx, rode camels, went up the Nile River by boat, saw dancing horses, watched the big ships go through the Suez Canal, and made new friends.

We did find that certain food items were simply not available at that time in the country. For example, donuts were impossible to find anywhere. We could find many wonderful pastries made by the local bakeries, but no one made donuts. Pancakes were not available either, but with a little shopping around and asking questions we found a solution. We bought crepe mix, mixed it much thicker than usual, and we had pancakes!

Hot dogs were a different story. Who would have thought that we wouldn't be able to grill or roast good old American style hot dogs? However, we found a solution to that as well. On certain nights, at special times and by invitation only, we could visit the American embassy in downtown Cairo. We could go to the Marine house and they would be roasting hot dogs. Needless to say, once discovered, we became very good friends with and frequent guests of the U.S. Marines!

All in all, it was a very good two years, but was also very hard on our family emotionally. It was a difficult decision for me to make. I was taking my two children far way while leaving everyone at home. My father and mother did not want me to go and missed me very much. They felt real heartache as they knew they could not travel to see me. As much as I had always moved around, they would always drive out to visit me every few months. This time it was beyond their capabilities to see me.

For me it was an experience I had never had or imagined. The country and customs were so different from any I had seen. The city itself was immense. Many people did not understand English. It took me many months before I could comprehend even basic Arabic.

I would drive the car myself in the evening after work rather than having the driver stay extra hours. There were a couple of times I was lost and had to ask many people for directions before getting back on course. In just driving around the city and realizing how deep the roots of this culture went, made me appreciate where I was now, the opportunity to learn, and how it was changing my perspective of the everyday routines I had in the U.S.

I was on an emotional high after climbing the pyramid as I had never experienced anything like that before. As days passed after the climb, I was almost shaking in my shoes when I thought about where we were and how quickly we could have been seriously injured.

At this point, I am truly amazed at the feat. I am not very comfortable at any height, and I could not even begin to make that climb today. Times when I'm faced with a challenge or needing to reach deep for courage, I think back to that day and what it took to climb up that pyramid, look over the edge some 500 feet to the bottom and step off. I am able to pull mental and physical strength from my core. Most of my challenges do not compare to that climb.

The experience of the President's assassination was terrifying. I could have been caught in crossfire between the shooters and the government forces, and I could have been killed in a split second. I was also very sad afterwards knowing the gravity of this act and what turmoil it would mean for the good people of Egypt.

My experiences in Egypt were in 1980 and 1981. Hosni Mubarak was Vice President. He had been standing next to the President during the parade and afterwards became President of Egypt. Now in 2011, as I write these words, he is no longer there and the country is again in turmoil.

There were many feelings of sadness from seeing the poor conditions under which many people lived. In some cases it looked as though the families were still living in biblical times. Whole families lived in very small huts amid primitive and dirty conditions. I saw wooden carts being pulled by donkeys with a father and son sitting on the small seat, the cart piled high with rubbish as they went down the road to the garbage dump. We were working in this area for a period of time so I had observed this often and realized they were working each day doing what they could just to survive.

The people I worked with and talked with during my two years in the country were very nice and were willing to help out. People went out of their way multiple times to help me or others, and never asked for, and generally would not accept any money for their assistance.

I did not fully realize or appreciate what great and profound experiences I had during the two year assignment in Egypt until I was back in the United States permanently. Each day as I was out shopping or at work, there would always be something that would strike me as different from what I was accustomed to. I found that my perception of daily events and the news from the papers and television was a little different than those around me. I realized that living in Egypt had shown me that there are different ways of doing things and one may not be right over the other; they are just different.

Questions for Reflection

1. What did you think of the decision making process I went through to go or not go on the assignment?

2. What other processes and considerations would you have taken into account?

3. Would you have involved your family and friends more deeply in the decision?

4. Considering all the adventures in Egypt described over the two year assignment, would you have gotten involved in all those activities?

5. What book or verses in the Bible would you have studied for this situation?

Chapter Five

A Wonderful Second Marriage

In the beginning of the book, I mentioned that one of my early experiences was a divorce after a short nine years of marriage and the birth of my wonderful children, a son and a daughter. Seeing my son and daughter grow and change from week to week during the nine years of marriage was one of the most wonderful periods of my life. With my wife's and my parting, the kids moved away with their mother to a different state. This was an exceptionally difficult time. Early one morning they loaded the car with clothes and other belongings. She started the car and slowly drove out the driveway. I was left with the memory of watching my young son and daughter peering out the back window of the car. It was a traumatic experience seeing them look back and wave to me without knowing why their dad was being left behind. I can still see those images in my head today, but I loved my children very much and stayed close to them through telephone calls and frequent visits.

After being divorced some nine years and moving halfway across the country, I met a wonderful lady that God brought into my life. I knew I couldn't lose her. We dated a short while and knew very quickly that we had something rare. It was as though we were made for each other and our outlook on life was as one.

I knew it was meant to be as too many things happened in a manner which ruled out mere coincidence. Both of us had moved around the country, living in many different states. I started out in Missouri and her in Pennsylvania. However, we both ended up in Colorado at the same time; her moving there from Oklahoma and me moving from Atlanta. I was an avid runner at the time and had started a new running club that met a couple of times per month. She was a runner and a friend of hers mentioned to her that she had recently heard of this new running club in town and gave her the contact number. That was me!

She called me, and we had a great conversation. Our next group run wasn't planned for several days, but I knew already I wanted to meet this lady so I asked her to meet me for a lunch time run the next week. I wanted to get acquainted with her and tell her more about the group and she agreed.

We had a good run, enjoyed talking during the run, and I could tell she was not just a jogger. She was a competitive runner and very fast. She joined our group for the next run and fit right in. We began dating after that, and she would come running with the group when she was back in town. It was somewhat difficult for us to date or for her to always run with us as she traveled a great deal. She did find time and we became very close. I knew in my heart I was in love with her.

When about three or four months had passed she informed me she would be out of town on an extended business trip. As I sat there and thought about this I knew I would miss her very much and was not looking forward to her being gone. In my heart, I knew that I loved her and needed to let her know how much she meant to me. I told her I loved her very much, did not want her to be away, and asked her to marry me! She said yes.

In just a few short days she had our wedding planned and the date was set. We were married in an outdoor ceremony at a beautiful resort in the foothills of Pikes Peak in Colorado. We created our wedding vows together with the minister. I believe the vows were inspired and meant to publicly state to our family and the world how we felt; that we were deeply in love and were being joined as one.

From the first part of the vows – "It is possible for a civilized man and woman to be happy in marriage, although if this is to be the case, a number of conditions must be fulfilled: There must be a feeling of complete equality on both sides; there must be no interference with mutual freedom; there must be the most complete mental intimacy; and there must be a certain similarity in regard to standards of values. Given all these conditions, I believe marriage to be the best and most important relation that can exist between two human beings" (from Bertrand Russell).

From the last section of our vows – "Now you will feel no rain, for each of you will be shelter for the other; now you will feel no cold, for each of you will be warmth for the other; now there will be no loneliness for you, for although you are two persons, there is but one life between you" (taken from the Apache).

We took this to heart and even though we certainly have individual likes, dislikes, opinions, and our own areas of interest, we spend a lot of time together and carefully consider each other's wishes.

During the years of our marriage I have learned a lot from my wife about being more compassionate and being more understanding of other people. My wife has shown me what it really means to care for and love dogs, how to appreciate nature and see beauty in trees and flowers. I had always had dogs as pets during childhood but didn't really understand them or appreciate them until seeing the care and love my wife had for them. When we lived in Colorado, we had two dogs. Then when we moved to Minnesota we were not able to buy a house immediately so we had to give both dogs away. It was difficult for me, but I saw that it was a much greater emotional strain for my wife. It was like giving a child up. That was the first time it really hit me as to how a person and a pet could form such a close and loving bond.

After a year or so, we moved into a property that allowed pets, so my wife found a young adult dog named Harry that we adopted from a foster home. I watched as she formed a bond with Harry and he became a part of our family. I grew to love him and understand him. After several years he began to have difficulties and we made frequent trips to the vet. Finally came the worst news; he had cancer and very little could be done.

With the fight he put up at the end coupled with the experiences we had as a family during the good years, my love and bond to dogs grew exponentially.

After his passing, followed by a long period of sadness, my wife decided that it would be best for us to consider adopting another dog. We went to the local pound to merely look, but after viewing several dogs and walking one, I heard my wife say to the shelter worker, "we will take him!" That's when we added Dax, a one year old 85 pound Labrador mix with high energy to our family. Dax was also very unique; he was tall, long legged, black and brindle with a narrow black strip of hair down the middle of his back, and very loving.

He really needed some work as he was scared and was extremely high energy. My wife showed the love and compassion she has for animals by spending every evening after work walking with him, teaching him how to heel, stop on command and many other things that he had just never been taught. We enrolled him in an obedience class at the shelter where we adopted him and after a few weeks of training he was a wonderful, manageable dog. The lady from the shelter came to us at the end of the training and thanked us for keeping him. I said she was welcome but didn't she mean thanks for adopting him? As many high energy dogs are returned, she replied no, thanks for *keeping* him.

How this affected me and what I learned-

The move to Colorado Springs and the two years I lived there proved to be not only a huge adventure and broadening of my knowledge but also a life changing experience.

I moved to Colorado to work with the Federal Business Sector of the company I had been with for many years. However, it would be completely different since this was a special project assignment for a classified project building a new satellite communication center for the U.S. Department of Defense. I was to be a project manager for a portion of the project and would be required to have a top secret security clearance. I was very excited to get started. I would be working with a select group of people and would be granted access to many special facilities.

During the time on the project, I had occasion to visit or spend some time in government facilities such as Cheyenne Mountain Colorado (NORAD) Vandenburg AFB California, (the SLC 7 space shuttle launch complex), the Blue Cube Satellite Control Center in California, White Sands Testing Range, Los Alomos Laboratory and the Kennedy Space Center in Florida.

The experiences during this time were incredible and left me with many great and exciting memories that forever changed my perspective on our world and space. However, I did not expect to meet the fantastic lady that would become my wife and how joining our lives would forever change me in all respects for the better.

My wife has had many impacts on me in addition to the deep respect and love for dogs that I now have. My wife's a very masterful gardener and has a fantastic eye for planning and creating an amazing environment for us at home. The planning and work she has done with the landscaping around our home is truly wonderful. A walk around the property leaves me in a calm and peaceful state of mind and encourages me to sit down for a few minutes and enjoy life. She has helped me relax and reflect, to better understand the ways of our pets, plants and other people.

My wife also broadens my views. She made me aware of how different we all are from one another and the decisions we make each day are based on our makeup or personality. She shared the need to pause at each of the complications and issues we encounter in our lives before passing judgment or criticizing others.

I had always been very aware of how my body was reacting and feeling as a result of my exercise and sports activities. What I did not realize and understand was how they were so closely connected to the understanding of my mind, thoughts, associations and interpretations of events, and the influences they have on my opinion and perceptions of others beliefs and actions.

I found that I was often so caught up in everything I had going on in my life that I did not consider what the other person might be struggling with in their life. Over the years I have learned to consider what other people are thinking and the burdens they are carrying. I now stop for a moment to reflect and consider others circumstances. It has me saying thanks to God for what I have in my life and gives me a more realistic way of thinking and dealing with the challenges in my life.

It may seem shocking that we were married after knowing each other only five months. But now after 22 amazing years of marriage, I can say that five months is just a number and we are right together. We truly do share the strength and bond between us as a couple joined together as one.

When you are in love, when things are right, when you are positive and have a smile on your face: the colors of the rainbow are brighter, the sun is warmer, the grass and trees are greener and the music of the wind and the birds singing is sweeter.

Questions for Reflection

1. Does the short period of dating shock or surprise you? What did you expect the outcome to be?

2. How does this compare to your personal experience or to someone you know?

3. Did any of the words in the wedding vows bring any specific thoughts to you?

4. Take a few minutes to reflect on life lessons you may have learned and internalized from experiences with people, pets or nature.

Chapter Six

September 11, 2001

During 2001 I was working for a company based in Minnesota, and I would travel both locally and out of state to meet clients. In the fall of 2001, I was looking at some opportunities in the St. Louis area and began to plan a trip there for meetings. As I planned for specific meetings and projects, I thought it would make sense to team with a second firm and have us **travel** at the end of August or first part of September. As I continued the discussions with the potential client and talked with the representative of our partner firm, we decided on a meeting in September and our partner firm would fly the two of us down there in their private airplane.

On the morning of September 11th, 2001, more commonly known as 9/11, we left Minnesota for St Louis. We were in the air on that fateful day during the first attacks on the World Trade Center in New York by terrorists using high jacked airplanes. The news of this attack, the timing, the sheer magnitude and emotional impact of the news was so overwhelming it was difficult to comprehend what happened and the ramifications.

The fact that I was actually in the air aboard a small private airplane during the attacks made it even more unbelievable and frightening to me. During the flight we heard some very brief news on the regular AM/FM radio regarding airplanes. We also received some rather strange commands from the air traffic controllers that made us wonder what had happened. Due to poor reception on the radio from a commercial news station, we only heard a few broken words that mentioned airplanes, other airplanes and the Pentagon. We were at a loss as to what the news could be about. We could only catch a word or two then it would cut out. Then the pilot called the air traffic controller for flight information to see if there was anything unusual taking place. The answer was very curt; we were to confirm that we were landing and this would be our stopping point. Now we were very concerned as this was far different than any conversation we had ever heard in flight instructions.

As we were approaching the airport in St Louis we were instructed by the air traffic controller to land full stop and to confirm more than once, that this was our final destination. We could not wait to land, get out of the airplane and find out what had happened; little did we know how serious and life changing this would be.

As soon as we landed we asked what had happened. We were told that planes had crashed into the Twin towers in New York City, one large commercial plane in each and a third airplane had hit The Pentagon. We were told that one plane was still in the air scheduled to land in California and was believed to be hijacked too. No one knew at this point where it might be headed. All other air traffic was being grounded and put on hold.

At this point we did not know how widespread this attack might be, and many terrible thoughts went through our minds. We were a long way from our home and families and didn't know if we or our families might be in danger.

It was a short time before we had a chance to see media coverage on TV and the unbelievable images of the planes crashing into the Twin Towers.

We sat stunned for an hour just watching the news on the TV in the airport. We talked with a few other people there and all were at a loss of what to do or say. We wondered what else might happen in the next few hours or days, and what we should do. Still in shock, we went back to our hotel and made certain we still had rooms and that we could stay a night or two longer if needed. I called my wife to see if she had heard the news and to see how she was dealing with the situation with myself out of town and no way back!

The rest of the day was spent thinking about what this would mean, why it happened and what the future held for the United States, the world and us. We attempted to get clearance to fly out but could not. All air traffic in the United States was grounded; as far I know this was the first time in history this had been ordered. We then wondered what else might be difficult; would the communications or banking functions be impacted as well. What if we needed money, would the networks still be up for credit card processing or to get cash from the ATM machines. In the mid afternoon I used the ATM in the hotel to get some cash in case it was needed.

We ended up staying overnight and into midday the next day as all flights were grounded, and we were probably going to be stranded for awhile since our private airplane would be a low priority to release. We checked on rental cars and there were none available. There were so many people stranded by this situation that all available rental cars from every agency were already rented or reserved.

After much discussion amongst the three of us, we decided we could possibly find a low cost used car to buy, share the expense and drive home.

We called a cab and spent three or four hours checking the used car lots before finally finding a car that was inexpensive and might actually make it all the way back to Minneapolis from St. Louis! We asked the dealer to thoroughly check the car over and make some repairs so it would be ready. We made a deal and agreed we would come back when they had the car repaired and ready to go.

We were absolutely in shock for the rest of that day and all night. I remember thinking how this could possibly happen, and what would the impact be to our county, economy, daily functioning, jobs, banks, and Wall Street. Might this only be the beginning of a larger scale attack on the United States? What might the next target be? How can I get back home to be with my family, and what if there was a separate attack there while I was still out of town? I really wondered what the future held for all of us.

After meeting for breakfast that second day, the three of us again discussed what was the best thing to do. We checked on the used car and it would be ready for pick up by the end of the day. We decided then we would get ready to go, leave our airplane there at the airport and start the drive back late in the afternoon around dark.

We headed out of St. Louis on I-70, on to Columbia, then turned north on Highway 63 to take a short cut back to Minneapolis. We went north and on through Kirksville where my parents and I would often go shopping when we lived in that area and where my aunts, uncles and cousins still live. We continued on north passing a few miles from Unionville, Missouri, where I graduated from high school and was President of my senior class at Unionville High.

Finally after a long night on the road and several pit stops, we were back in Minneapolis. After picking my car up at the airport, I drove home in the early morning thinking how happy I would be to see my wife and the conversations we would have.

How this affected me and what I learned-

With many uncertain feelings and how the trip would go during the long drive, it actually was a soothing and settling experience driving back through northern Missouri where I grew up. This long, solemn trip during the night and early morning hours gave me some reassurance seeing the farms, the farm houses, barns and fields that were so familiar to me. They took me back to memories from a simpler time when I was a young boy growing up. I was born in the area and lived there until I was 20 years of age. I always remember feeling comfortable in rural areas as I was raised on the farm and spent many hours driving a tractor while working in the fields with my father.

I clearly remember that at that point in time the very familiar images and memories from many years ago gave me great comfort and helped restore calmness in me. Just days before, my core strength had been shaken to the core but now my faith and core strength were nourished and rebuilt.

I believe that I will forever have the thoughts and memories of the World Trade Center's Twin Towers and other scenes from the media coverage in my mind. Not too many years before 2001, I had stood on the outdoor viewing deck of one of those towers and thought how great it would be to live and work in one of them. As God would have it, that did not come to pass or I might not have lived to be able to tell this story.

Questions for Reflection

1. What thoughts or strong emotions come to your mind from this event?

2. Do you have a special connection to someone that was there?

3. How did this tragic event impact or affect you?

4. What Bible reading or passages gave you or could have given you the most comfort during this time?

Chapter Seven

Major Back Problems

Like many of us in the world today, I had back pain starting in my late 30's and early 40's. I had always been active so I am not certain when the level of pain actually became a problem, but it was a low level nuisance before it became a major issue. I did not start running until I was 40 years old to relieve stress. After a few months running causally, my competitive drive kicked in. After that, I worked very hard to get better and faster. I started with 5K and 10K races and trained to get personal records each race. I ran a number of races and joined a local running group during the time I lived in Atlanta.

My company then transferred me from Atlanta to Colorado Springs. I continued my running there and moved up to marathons and ultra marathons. I had developed a great deal of endurance by running in the foothills and into the mountains in the area. I developed more speed through a program mapped out for me by the U.S. Olympic training center in Colorado Springs.

I continued to run during the time in Colorado and had very few issues with injuries.

My wife and I moved to Minneapolis after a short time in Colorado and I continued to run there. I also participated in snowshoe racing.

As I ran more and more, the pain increased but was still not a major issue. However, it came to a breaking point when I ran a 24 hour race and completed 72 miles. About three weeks after that, I ran the Twin Cities Marathon which is when I really started feeling the pain every day. It was at a level that slowed me down when merely walking.

The pain was there all the time and was draining my energy. I would take a daily dose of over the counter medication and would still come home after work and just lie down on the floor to get some relief. I was so tired I would go to bed early but find little relief upon rising.

Eventually I knew I had to do something and made an appointment with a doctor. Over the course of many months, I ended up seeing a variety of doctors from M.D.'s to chiropractors to physical therapists.

The doctors had prescribed various pain medications and I still wasn't getting relief. The pain medications were very low level and did allow me to function on a limited basis. I knew that I did not want to be on any pain medications for an extended period of time and certainly did not want to get into a higher level of pain medication. I knew in my heart this problem could be fixed. I had to manage my mind in order to control the pain and ignore the high levels of pain and difficulty in walking.

There were times when I would be walking and the pain level would reach the point where I could not walk. I would have to stop for a few minutes to adjust to the pain, and then continue walking. I was at an end as to what to do but did not want to accept the life changing event that I knew was in front of me.

In my quest to find relief, get rid of this life altering problem, and continue with running, I actually asked one of the doctors if he could just remove my leg, fit me with an artificial one and let me get back to running.

As it turned out, I am very fortunate the doctors did not take me up on this as the problem **was not with my leg** but was in fact a problem with a disc in my lower back. After changing doctors and a couple of very detailed tests later, a neurosurgeon fixed the problem with an operation.

This was a great relief, and it let me get on with my life. Unfortunately, it was the end of my running.

How this affected me and what I learned-

Needless to say, at the very least this slowed my life down and prevented me from participating in a lot of activities. Before the operation, I really had to manage the pain more with my mind than with any medication. I had never been one to take medications, especially pain medications.

Now the management was of a different nature. I no longer had the pain but was left with the sinking realization that my life had forever changed. I could certainly never get back to the level of running that I had enjoyed before, and the very real possibility existed that I would never run again. How could I adjust to that? I ran for relaxation. I enjoyed the feeling of going on a run in the evenings and on the weekends to relax. I took pleasure in the feeling of being outdoors with the wind blowing in my face as I ran with the freedom to let my mind wander and meditate. Running had been a method of relaxation for me and I was involved in competitions for several years. I had spent a great deal of time, effort and hard training to reach where I was.

After several months of feeling lost, I knew that I had to find a replacement for my running. I no longer had a hobby and was lost after work when I had newly freed up time. It was difficult to see others training and racing in 5k and 10k races during the summer. I knew I had to find something to get me involved, fuel my need for fun and bring back the enjoyment of the comradeship of being a part of a special group or club.

Then one day I noticed a very nice, bright red sports car driving by and that reminded me of my love for cars that I had since I was a very young boy. I then began to take notice of sports cars on the road as I was driving to work. Then one day I saw a red Porsche sitting alongside a house in the neighborhood with a for sale sign on it! I had to stop. It was a beautiful, used, red Porsche and was very reasonably priced. I looked it over, talked with the owner and promised to call him in a day or two after I had talked with my wife. She was very supportive as she knew I needed a hobby to keep me sane and out of her way. The next weekend I was the proud owner of the red car.

As it turned out, this was the focus I needed. It provided my life with balance and kept me happy between working a job that required a lot of travel and having a fun hobby that would get me involved with good friends.

Little did I know just how big this second childhood would be, starting with this first sports car after many years.

Questions for Reflection

1. Have you had a similar experience or thoughts?

2. This challenge was a life changing event for me; would you have made different decisions?

3. This was both a painful physical and mental process that lasted a couple of years. What other steps could you think of that might have been easier or better?

4. Reflect on this change in life. How in giving up running led me to a new hobby with cars and the old saying "when one door closes, a new one opens". Do you have any situations where this might apply?

Chapter Eight

Learning from a heart attack

Each of our personal experiences and life challenges will certainly be different from one another as well as different to us as individuals from our other challenges.

With my heart attack, it was totally different from any challenge before or after. It came on quickly and totally unexpected. I had no real indications that I was at a high risk other than an elevated cholesterol level.

I was exercising at a health club regularly and had not experienced any issues. Then one day I went back to the office after working out and within an hour I began experiencing chest discomfort and an upset stomach. They seemed much different than any physical symptoms I had before. I would get up and walk around but still could not get relief. Meanwhile, the odd feeling I had could not be explained.

After a short time, I left the office to walk around town thinking fresh air would help. As I thought through the options as to what might be wrong, I did think of the possibility of a heart attack. I then entered a drug store and made my way to the pharmacy. After a few minutes, I talked with the pharmacist and asked him if he thought it might be a heart attack and if so, should I take an aspirin. He said he could not tell me but asked if I had shooting pains. I said no. He asked if I had a feeling of a band around my chest making it difficult to breath; again, I said no. He asked if I felt light headed. I said no. He then said, well, I do not know but you should go to the emergency room to be checked. I bought a bottle of aspirin and took one before I left the store.

I walked slowly back to the office and wondered if I really could be having a heart attack. Nothing had really changed in the last half hour or so, but I did seem to feel a pressure in my chest. It was a feeling I had never had before and it concerned me. I began to question now what might be wrong and how serious this could be. I just could not imagine what it would mean to have a heart attack and how this might change my life. Would I survive, would I be severely impaired, could I lead any part of a normal life even if I did live through this?

I walked back in the office and a coworker asked if I was okay. I described how I felt and they said they would drive me to the hospital if I wanted to go. As we talked, I noticed that the pressure in my chest had increased and I could feel pressure that felt to be in the middle of my back. At this time, my boss came to me and told me to go into the conference room because we needed to have a quick meeting. I told him I didn't think I could make it because I may be having a heart attack! He looked at me in total disbelief. I briefly explained to him how I felt and thought that I really should go have this checked out. He agreed but did not think it was serious.

He later came up to the hospital to check on me to see why he had not heard any news. He had been certain that my illness was only temporary and I would be just fine. He was very surprised when he checked in with the front desk and they informed him that I had in fact suffered a heart attack, and they could not treat it there. I had been transported by ambulance to a hospital specializing in heart issues.

Fortunately, I made it to the hospital in time and the doctors were standing by for my arrival. I recovered from the attack and the procedure that followed. I was released to go home in only a couple of days. I was back to normal.

How this affected me and what I learned-

This was a learning experience that was different from any other. During the attack, I really realized how fragile life is. I had left home that morning as any other morning thinking it was a regular day. However, as I lay on the table in the hospital while suffering a heart attack, I realized that I might not go home that night.

I remember being surprised that my life could end right there amongst strangers; while my coworkers, friends and family went on about their business. I wondered how they would take the news, how they would react, and what they would say.

I wondered how my wife would handle the news, and I was heartbroken over the fact I might not see her again or have the chance to tell her good bye and that I loved her. Where were my son and daughter and how would they react. I would not have a chance to tell them good bye either.

Then I thought about our dog, Harry our beloved adopted Spring Spaniel I was almost always home from work before my wife and our dog expected me to be there every night to pet and feed him. Who would feed him tonight?

After I was released from the hospital, I felt very relieved to be on my feet again and to be going home. However, this was different. As soon as I was outside the hospital, I felt a moment of panic. I was calmed knowing that I knew God was with me through this experience and I had excellent care in the hospital. I knew that someone could be at my bedside in a moment or two if I really needed assistance, but now I was outside. What if I was on a trip by myself and needed help, would someone respond in time?

Fortunately I was able to dig into my core being and faith, and convince myself that this was not likely to happen, and if it did I surely would get help. I will never forget the lesson that life is very uncertain and it can change or end at anytime without any warning.

I did pray to God often, and thank him for getting me through this experience, and my faith carried me through the crisis until I became comfortable in leading a normal life once again. It makes me think about how precious each day is and how we should be thankful for every moment we have.

Questions for Reflection

1. Have you or someone close to you had a similar experience?

2. What were the emotions involved?

3. What prayers would you have prayed to God?

4. What readings or other support methods were most effective?

Chapter Nine

Learning from Cancer

I have always been very active, enjoyed being outdoors, working in the yard, being involved with cars and participating in competitive sports. I was a runner starting at age 40 and started participating thereafter in races from one mile (running a best of 5:00 for the mile and 3:06 for a marathon) to running a 72 mile ultra marathon.

After my back problems, I was unable to continue my running. I always enjoyed cars, so I left the running scene behind and bought a used Porsche and began entering various driving events, including autocross and then drivers sessions at the high speed road course tracks. I really enjoyed this from a high excitement perspective as well as the close camaraderie with other drivers, so I signed up for training sessions with driving instructors and eventually became a driving instructor myself.

From there I knew I was hooked, and before long I began driving race cars and competing in road course events at really great tracks including Brainerd Raceway in Minnesota, Road America in Wisconsin, Autobahn in Joliet, Illinois, Mid Ohio in Ohio and I even raced my car at Daytona International in Florida. By now my wife and I had moved to Chicago and I had access to even more car events.

I watched my health, listened to my body and had health checkups regularly. I appeared to be in great health.

Then life threw me a curve.

At the end of 2007 we were visiting our daughter and her family for Christmas. I was having some issues with certain foods causing digestive problems and had to be very selective with the food I ate over the holidays. Then at the beginning of the new year I was having more digestive issues. I had noticed difficulty digesting certain spicy foods in the previous couple months and was now having difficulty with other oily or high fiber foods.

I then knew that something was not normal when this had been going on for too long. I scheduled an appointment with my doctor, and he said it was most likely a sensitivity I had developed to certain foods due to my age. For the next few weeks I really watched my food selections and eliminated all spicy, fried or oily foods. My situation improved minimally. On the second visit to the doctor, he asked how long it had been since my last colonoscopy. I said six years and he scheduled one for me as soon as possible.

My wife had a weekend conference scheduled downtown Chicago the last weekend in May, and I planned to go with her for the weekend. My colonoscopy test was scheduled to take place on that Friday.

After I woke up from the test, I asked the doctor as soon as I saw him for the results or how long it would be before he would know. He said sir, you have cancer. I was taken aback. I knew something wasn't right, but I had never suspected that it might be cancer. I knew nothing about cancer. No one in our family had ever even had any type of cancer.

I asked if they had to send a specimen in for testing to be certain and doctor said that they certainly would do that but he had enough experience to know that this was cancer.

My wife and I were hit very hard initially. At that point we really didn't know the full diagnosis, treatment options or what the full impact to me and our family would be. I had so many questions and I did not know what to do next. I thank God for my wonderful wife, her understanding, compassion, support and love.

We decided to go to the conference. I didn't want my wife to miss it and I really wanted to enjoy a weekend in Chicago while I felt alright not knowing what was ahead of me in the coming months. In fact, I was diagnosed with Stage 2 Colorectal Cancer.

The conference my wife was attending was an annual Oncology conference. How very fortunate we were to be able to collect booklets and pamphlets that contained helpful information from the conference. This started my education as to what I was really dealing with, what the outcome might be, and how to begin to understand and beat this challenge!

My doctors and specialists conferred and then met with my wife and me to discuss treatment options. They recommended an operation to be certain all the cancer was removed. Options included chemotherapy and radiation treatments, but they did not believe those alone would provide the best long term results. We decided to proceed with chemo and radiation treatments, followed by a six week break for my body to recover, and then schedule an operation. The doctors thought the operation would be fairly straightforward, but there were complications. The cancer was very low in my colon and would involve the rectal area.

I was referred to an Oncologist for chemo treatments, a doctor for radiation treatments and a surgeon. I drove over to the treatment center five days a week for the radiation treatments and they went well except for some discomfort and soreness the last week and a half. For the chemo, they set me up with an infusion pump that was attached to a waist belt. The pump was connected by a small tube to a "port a cath" that was installed in my upper chest area. That went well, except for times when I was playing with my dog in the yard and he would jump around playfully; his paw would sometimes accidently get caught in the plastic tubing, and we would be dancing around trying to get untangled without disconnecting the pump or breaking the tube!

After 25 radiation treatments and five weeks of around the clock chemo, additional tests were run and I had a break before the surgery in October. Unfortunately, the tests indicated that while the treatments had done their job, it was still questionable whether the operation might include a resection; removing a portion of my colon and re-attaching it, or if I would have a permanent colostomy with a pouch the rest of my life. The final decision would be made by the doctor during the operation with the outcome depending on the extent and location of the cancer relative to the colon and the rectal area.

I had the surgery in October and the cancer was removed. The surgery was slightly over four hours and without any complications. I did however have the permanent colostomy with the end of the colon being brought through the wall of my abdomen so I now wear a pouch. I have not found that to be an issue and I am very active again. I made an excellent recovery, although I did have to adjust my diet somewhat to aid in the healing and I do have sensitivity to certain foods. I did not have any pain issues other than a high level of sensitivity while sitting. Now that many months have passed, it all seems routine, except for the constant reminder that I will always wear a pouch.

How this affected me and what I learned-

The few months during healing and full recovery were really the very beginning of many changes in my life and were a critical turning point in my life. Even though I maintained a good appetite through those preceding months, I had lost 20 pounds, and I had no idea of where this journey would take me other than I had met many fine people. I had excellent doctors, had tremendous support, and really realized that life can throw some big changes at you at anytime. It made me rethink my life plan!

I should have been better informed earlier in my life. I was probably very lucky that I wanted to take care of myself and be able to participate in sports and competitive events for years to come. Knowing this drove me to ask questions and learn more about the treatments, options and what life would be like after my treatments, surgery and recovery.

Support from my family, friends, religion, church and handy informational pamphlets from the ACS regarding facts on how to mentally cope with the emotional thoughts were excellent. I also read inspirational books such as Lance Armstrong's book, <u>It's not about the Bike-My Journey back to Life</u>. I found humor and just laughing out loud to be very good for stress reduction.

This experience was really quite different from my heart attack. The process and time duration was different and there was a plan for treatment including many treatments and options, and I had the feeling that I would make it through but that my life would be forever changed, certainly more restricted and complicated. During the months of recovery after the chemo, radiation and surgery, I was at home and did not want to go anywhere. My son and daughter both traveled from their homes to spend a week each with me. My wife continued to work but was by my side and ever encouraging. My dog Dax was with me all day at home, and even though I started back to work part time very quickly after the operation, I somehow was different and wanted to stay close to home. Dax was a real friend and such a comfort to be around. I would work in my home office and he would be in his kennel in the lower level of the house. He would come up two or three times during the day, walk into my office and touch me with his nose to let me know he was with me and all was well. I would pat him on the head a couple of times before he would go back to his kennel.

Dax and I would walk two or three times a day; him for necessity, me just to get out of the house and enjoy the walk outdoors. Sometimes when I really needed a break or was just very tired, I would go into the living room and call Dax to come upstairs to spend some time together. He was always happy to come up and sit or lie down while I would talk to him, or sometimes read to him.

Even many months later, I am still coping with this odd sensation. I feel somewhat apprehensive anytime a trip is necessary, or even having to go a short distance for a day. I really feel a pull and strong desire to be back in my comfort zone which is in my house, in my neighborhood and in my local community. It is as though I need the routine and the familiarity of surroundings close by.

People are individuals, so during difficult times each of us should be aware of different methods of coping and find those that work best for us. During the times when your mind is thinking of all the issues and things that could go wrong, or those times when you find yourself awake at 2 am, you may need to read, take a walk, watch TV, listen to the radio, write in a journal, or simply count to yourself in order to occupy your mind. One important point of advice: do not let negative thinking take over your mind. If that happens, simply tell yourself to stop that thinking and set your mind to something different or relaxing.

Due to all the great support I received during my experience and all the wonderful people I met, I wanted to give back to the community. I wanted to share my experience and to get the message out to take care of yourself, be informed, have early and frequent checkups and keep a positive attitude.

I believe each person must be their own advocate to collect information, be informed, ask questions, ask why and why not and what the options are.

Questions for Reflection

1. Do any of the thoughts and reactions I described fall in line with feelings you would expect one to have?

2. What thoughts and issues do you have regarding this challenge?

3. I found in this challenge that humor was an excellent coping mechanism that worked very well and one that I had not used before. Reflect on what words of comfort you might use as listed in the toolbox in chapter ten.

4. How did this challenge impact and change your life or the life of someone you knew?

Chapter Ten

Sports and Life

You may wonder what sports have to do with a journey in faith and coping. I believe sports for me were an integral part of my make up, being, personality, ego, base foundation and a key part of my coping skills set. During the writing of this book, I realized that I had learned much and had pulled from my sports and competitive events to help me through difficult times in life, in business and in everyday life. Through my participation and competition in sports, I learned many things including discipline, training, how to best use my conscious and subconscious mind, how to focus, how to work with others, and how to use the mind and the body together, each supporting and inspiring the other.

While in elementary and even in high school, I was always active but not really involved in any organized sports. I did not believe that I was fast enough for the track team, big enough for football, quick enough for wrestling, nor strong enough to be a big hitter in baseball. Even in high school I probably never weighed more than 155 pounds. It was not until several years later that I became active in any real sports. In the following short stories I share three of my passions with you.

Running

At the age of 40, while living in Atlanta, Georgia, a friend introduced me to running. I really had no interest in running, but I was under significant stress from work due to long hours and deadlines. My friend suggested that running would reduce my stress and get me outdoors, which I always enjoyed.

In the next couple of weeks following our conversation, I bought a pair of running shoes, pulled on some shorts and an old T-shirt, and ran just two to three miles at a time. I remember thinking that this was going to be really easy for me. Well, big surprise! I found that even though I thought I was in good condition, I couldn't even run half a mile without being out of breath. I had never been a runner and did not do any walking other than what was required, so now this became quite the challenge. I was determined to find out what it would take to condition myself so that I could run a mile or two at a time. I learned quickly that it was best for me to run a short distance and extend it a little each time until I was really out of breath, then walk for awhile to recover, then run again, and repeat.

It didn't actually take too many days until I was doing much better and became more comfortable that I could run more than a mile without stopping. As soon as I could run a couple of miles, I discovered that is was a great deal of stress reduction occurs for me. Since I was running with the intention of reducing my stress, I would run at the end of the day when my stress had built up to a level of having a tight neck, back, and a headache. After two miles of running, the headache would be totally gone!

This hooked me. I have never been one to take any medications that I absolutely did not need. I found that this relieved my stress and I no longer had to take aspirin or any other over the counter meds.

As I began to talk to my friend about my running experiences, they said that I was actually making fantastic progress and I might want to run a 5k race. So at 40 years of age I entered my first running race. I had such a good time, and ran something just over 20 minutes. I was very encouraged by this to find I could actually complete a race, and that I was not last.

During that summer, I ran longer distances on the forest trails and found what was for me an excellent form of meditation. At first I would make a conscious effort to focus on the trail, the trees and outdoor sights. Then my mind would come back to an issue or deadline at work and I would have to put that out of my mind again and refocus on the trees and outdoor sights. After running 30 to 45 minutes and going through this exercise, my mind and body would relax and I would be in full enjoyment of the present moment and nature. I remember a couple of times where I was so enveloped in the present moment that as I came to the edge of the woods where the highway cut through the forest area and the cars were speeding by. I had to stop. I realized that I had no idea where I was, and that was a good thing! I got lost in the present moment.

Perhaps running in the early morning would have worked for me as well, but I was not an early riser and it definitely worked for me to run at the end of the day so I could actually feel the stress draining from my body and my mind relaxing. I was free from any time restraints because my work day was over and I did not have a schedule to follow.

I continued to run and began training to gain speed and build my confidence in 10k races. I had capitalized on an opportunity to run in the Peachtree 10k Road Race before I moved from Atlanta. The race was limited to 50,000 runners. It was quite the experience being lined up with everyone, standing there attempting to stay loose in a jammed area while waiting for the starting signal. My heart rate soared with all the excitement even before the race began. The excitement of the huge crowd, the course lined with masses of spectators and four or five news helicopters hovering overhead was enough to push the heart rate up to levels you would only expect to see during the actual race!

I became a fairly good runner and enjoyed racing in 5k and 10k races, as well as running in the evening for relaxation. A chance encounter after a race in downtown Atlanta led to a whole new experience in running and fun. After the race was over, I noticed a group of people running around in the park area. They were dressed like runners but they had on a few extra such things: caps, colorful shirts, bandannas, and a couple of runners were carrying banners and some sort of flag. They didn't seem to be taking part in the race to win or set a personal best, they were just running around, yelling and making a lot of noise. They really seemed to be having fun!

I had to just stop and see what this group was all about. As I watched them go by, I was looking to see if they were a club or some sort of organization. I could not really tell, but I heard several of them shouting, "on-on", several times and everyone seemed to keep repeating this. I had to know what this group was! They actually seemed to be good runners while having a great time simultaneously. I finally made contact with one of them and asked about the group. They told me they were a fun running group called the Atlanta Hash House Harriers!

History of the Hash

The Hash House Harriers is a decentralized organization with each chapter, sometimes called a kennel, individually managed with no uniting organizational hierarchy (although the locations of national and international gatherings are decided by a meeting involving representatives from a number of hashes). A chapter's management is typically known as the MisManagement and consists of individuals with various duties and titles. There are more than 1,700 chapters spanning all seven continents. Most major cities are home to at least one chapter. Chapters typically contain between 20-100 members, usually mixed-sex, with some metropolitan area Hashes drawing more than 1,000 hashers to an event.

Hashing originated in December 1938 in Kuala Lumpur, then in the Federated Malay States (now Malaysia), when a group of British colonial officers and expatriates began meeting on Monday evenings to run, in a fashion patterned after the traditional British Paper Chase or "Hare and Hounds", to rid themselves of the excesses of the previous weekend.

After meeting for some months, they were informed by the Registrar of Societies that as a "group," they would require a Constitution and an official name. A. S. Gispert suggested the name "Hash House Harriers" after the Selangor Club Annex, where the men were billeted, known as the "Hash House" for its notoriously monotonous food. Apart from the excitement of chasing the hare and finding the trail, harriers reaching the end of the trail would be rewarded with beer, ginger beer and cigarettes.

The Constitution of the Hash House Harriers is recorded on a club registration card dated 1950:
- To promote physical fitness among our members
- To get rid of weekend hangovers
- To acquire a good thirst and to satisfy it in beer
- To persuade the older members that they are not as old as they feel

Hashing died out during World War II after the invasion of Malaya, but was re-started after the war by most of the original group, minus A. S. Gispert, who was killed on 11 February 1942 in the Japanese invasion of Singapore, an event commemorated by many chapters by an annual Gispert Memorial Run.

Apart from a "one-off" chapter formed on the Italian Riviera by Gus Mackie, growth of Hashing remained small until 1962, when Ian Cumming founded a chapter in Singapore. The idea then spread through the Far East, Europe, Australia, and New Zealand, and North America, booming in popularity during the mid-1970s.

At present, there are almost two thousand chapters in all parts of the world, with members distributing newsletters, directories, and magazines and organizing regional and world Hashing events. As of 2003, there are even two organized chapters operating in Antarctica.

Most chapters gather on a weekly or monthly basis, though some events occur sporadically, e.g. February 29th, Friday the 13th, or a full moon.

At a Hash, one or more members (Hares) lay a trail, which is then followed by the remainder of the group (the Pack or Hounds). The trail periodically ends at a "check" and the pack must find where it begins again; often the trail includes false trails, short cuts, dead ends, back checks and splits. These features are designed to keep the pack together regardless of fitness level or running speed, as front-runners are forced to slow down to find the "true" trail, allowing stragglers to catch up.

Members often describe their group as "a drinking club with a running problem," indicating that the social element of an event is as important, if not more so, than any athleticism involved. Beer remains an integral part of a Hash, though the balance between running and drinking differs between chapters, with some groups placing more focus on socializing and others on running.

Generally, Hash events are open to the public and require no reservation or membership, but some may require a small fee, referred to as hashcash, to cover the costs incurred, such as food or drink.

The end of a trail is an opportunity to socialize, have a drink and observe any traditions of the individual chapter (see Traditions). When the Hash officially ends, many members may continue socializing at an On-After, On-Down, On-On-On, Apres, *or Hash Bash, an event held at a nearby house, pub, or restaurant. ("Hash House Harriers." Wikipedia. Wikimedia Foundation, Aug. 2009. Web. 09 Apr. 2012. http://en.wikipedia.org/wiki/Hash_House_Harriers).*

It was in Colorado Springs, Colorado, that I established a local chapter of the Hash House Harriers after being transferred there to work on a government communications project. I named this group the Pikes Peak Hash House Harriers or PPH4 as we typically met in the general area at the base of Pikes Peak.

The other unique quality of this group is that anyone that came back and ran with them more than a few times would then be given a really crazy nickname that the group would make up. This ceremony would be done at the end of a run after the group had a chance to know the person and to find out some wild stories or perhaps anything that could provide ideas for a wild nickname. Of course, they did not name the person until after a few beers had been consumed, making it even more interesting. A typical Hasher group would be made up of people from every walk of life and occupation. A group could contain attorneys, medical personnel, carpenters and builders, business owners, military personnel and others. Often the nickname given to someone would be based on their profession, a personality trait or habit they would have. Oh, one more thing; we tried very, very hard to make certain the nickname selected was as embarrassing as possible! I continued to run with this group for many months and also participated in training and actual races.

The move to Colorado Springs was a great experience, new people, new running friends, excellent scenic trails to run, and the Pikes Peak Mountain of 14,110 feet altitude. I ran the trails in the foothills of Pikes Peak; one of the magnificent "fourteeners" (a mountain in excess of 14,000 feet altitude) in Colorado. It was inspiring!

I started running the foothills and planned to run a short distance up Pikes Peak, but for some reason I felt slower and almost felt as though I had an extra 50 pounds on my back. As I ran shorter distances and ran easier, I asked the other runners why it was so different. They told me it was not only the hilly terrain but mainly due to the altitude. Even at the base area of the mountain, we were at about 5,000 feet above sea level. They said it could take as long as six months to get acclimated to the change.

After a couple of months I entered a 5k race, and sure enough, even though I ran hard, my time was much slower than my previous 5k races in Georgia. I continued to work at this for about six months before my times met my previous times. That was an accomplishment, after having gone backwards for a period of time. Finally my hard work paid off. I went to Atlanta and ran a 5k race. It was so easy! I set a new personal best for a 5k distance. After running for more than six months at high altitude, the air was so much better at sea level. I actually ended up running a 5k in Atlanta in the 17 minute range!

I went back to Colorado and continued to practice and work on my speed. It really felt good to be able to run at the faster pace. I had never been that fast. I also began running longer distances upon meeting some new friends that were Ultra distance runners in 50 to 100 mile runs. The longer runs helped build strength which helped my 5k and 10k races.

Then through a chance meeting and conversation with some other athletes in town, I learned about the Olympic Training center located in Colorado Springs, and that I might be able to get into a training program with them. I hooked up with a coach there that set up a program to focus on my one mile base speed. Through an extensive testing program involving treadmill work, VO2 Max testing and blood lactic acid testing, they helped determine my capabilities for a one mile distance. They also taped this test. It is very interesting to me now to be able to go back and watch the video of me on the treadmill with all the wires and hoses connected to me and truly appreciate how very cool this was. And it worked!

We set a goal for the end of summer for me to run a mile in five minutes flat. They convinced me that the tests indicated that I had the lung capacity and blood capabilities to process the lactic acid buildup to allow a five minute mile. So, believing in them, the tests and the training program, I set out to reach my new goal.

I trained hard and teamed up with other runners that would test and support me in the training. We trained several weeks out before a race.

The day of my next race, I asked my coach how I should run the mile event. He said, "here is the strategy: run the first quarter at this pace, then the second quarter at this pace, then the third quarter at this pace, then just run flat out as hard as you can for the last quarter!" Not quite what I had expected and I expressed my concern that perhaps I was not ready to go that hard. Maybe we were maybe being a little too ambitious. He asked if I did the training and I said yes. He said very matter of factly, "Well, then you can do the event."

I started the race determined to do what I had trained my mind and body to do. I ran hard and it was as though I was running on automatic, just as I had trained. I crossed the finish line, at the age of 44, with an official time of 5:00.00 and a personal best.

How this affected me and what I learned-

I learned that you have to believe; believe in yourself and in others around you. I learned to first ask for help and then put your trust in those helping.

My new experiences of training for and running long distance races, including Ultra-Marathons, with the barriers of altitude and terrain, put me in very good physical shape and strengthened my mind. I learned how to focus my mind on running hard and how to relax and enjoy the scenery while the subconscious mind handled the details when running on difficult trails, up and down Pikes Peak with uneven terrain, loose gravel and rocks.

My experience in training for the one mile competition instilled in me a confidence in planning, setting goals, believing, working hard, and believing in a process of the mind and body working together.

Snowshoe Racing

After a couple of years in Colorado Springs, my wife and I moved to Minneapolis, Minnesota. I continued my running there from 5k and 10k races to the Twin Cities Marathon and a trip to Chicago to run the Chicago marathon. I also did a 24 hour run in Minnesota where I was fortunate enough to complete 72 miles.

Then the next winter I started training on lightweight, aluminum, racing snowshoes. It was a great way to train in the winter with the enjoyment of being outdoors. Before that I had done some winter training by running inside at the metro dome.

The snowshoe training was a lot of fun and hard work. But I really enjoyed it. Of course, I then had to compete in races. I ran a 5k and a 10k and did quite well. One of the races was rather memorable due to the amount of snow and the temperature being ten below! I parked as close as I could to the starting line, got out and warmed up with heavy clothes on. Then at the last minute, just before the start of the race, I took off the heavy coat and just had on racing tights, a heavy cap and big gloves. We ran the race and I was never cold. In fact, I was hot! So I quickly walked back to the car and put on my heavy clothes so I would not turn into an icicle.

However, that was not the craziest thing I did while on snowshoes. The next summer, my wife and I traveled to Colorado for a snowshoe race in the great sand dunes in the San Louis Valley. What a beautiful place; great mounds of giant sand dunes that looked like smaller versions of the Rocky Mountains range. In this particular location, these great sand dunes that covered a huge area were also completely surrounded by a ring of real mountains. The great sand dunes were created by the winds coming down from the mountains on one side, picking up large amounts of sand and carrying it across the valley before depositing it on the far side.

We went out a couple of days before the race so we could do some sightseeing and I could practice for the race. I was fascinated by the vast area and expanse of the sand. It really looked like a real mountain range. They were very tall at differing heights and looked just like other mountains. As I ran, I would go up one side, down the other, up the next one, and down the other. I was always looking for the highest peak. The snowshoes would dig into the sand as I ran, making it hard work to run. As I lifted my foot up, the tip of the snowshoe would dig into the sand and it would seem harder than running in the sand with only shoes on. Coming down a dune was a real blast. The snowshoes would almost float on top allowing me to take very long strides. Then when the snowshoe would hit, it would stay on top of the sand and slide down the slope. It was a sensation of floating or having winged feet!

As I ran my way up to the dune's peak, I felt as though I was going up into the sky; it was perfectly clear and a brilliant blue. When I finally reached the highest peak, I just sat down in the sand and listened to the wind blowing around the dunes. I remember thinking how peaceful this was.

The race was that weekend and my wife and I went out early in the morning to check in and have time to walk around. Then it was time to put the snowshoes on, warm up and stretch. The race was well attended. Many people had traveled significant distances to participate in the unique event.

I had a great day and ran a great race. I ran hard, finished strong and won my age group. The prize was a real nice pair of hiking boots!

How this affected me and what I learned-

During a practice run, when I was out in the dunes alone, I ran and climbed until I was at the highest peak in the sand dunes. I sat down on the very top in one spot by myself for a long time just meditating on the beauty, the silence and how God created all of this and only a few have been fortunate enough to experience it.

I remember thinking back as far as I could while I was sitting there, just trying to get back to when I was a young kid, back to the very earliest age I had any trace of memory. I think I got as far back as the age of four. I spent some time there reflecting and going back, back to a point where I had no memory really but then trying to imagine what it could have been like. It was truly a very spiritual experience. I came away from the peak of that sand dune with a new perspective.

Cars

It was during high school and a college that I realized I had an interest in learning all about cars. This interest went back to me attending car racing at the local county fairs with my parents when I was very young, probably no more than seven or eight years of age. We would go to the county fairgrounds to watch the dirt track racing with stock cars and the daredevils driving new cars and performing daring driving maneuvers such as jumping ramps, driving up on two wheels, crisscrossing with multiple cars and performing precision synchronized driving.

In high school I was old enough to get my driver's license and have my own car. My first car was a 1955 Chevy. Certainly it was one of the classics. It was a two door hardtop in really great condition. I really do owe my parents one for that. As I drove the car and got a feel for it, I thought about what I wanted to do to truly make it my car. All I ending up doing to the car was changing it from an automatic to a stick. From there it was a natural jump to want them to handle better and run faster.

I enjoyed the sounds, the competition, meeting new people, sharing ideas and the pure enjoyment of owning, tuning and competing with my own car.

I was able to indulge in my passion for cars for a few years after high school by buying a 1957 Chevy after the 55, then a 1962 Chevy SS (Super Sport) with the 300 horsepower engine but with an automatic transmission. I really liked that car, but I knew I needed a 4 speed to really enjoy it. Soon the opportunity came to trade the automatic for a 4 speed car. Other than the trans, the cars were identical. I really liked shifting the gears with the 4 speed. Then by 1965 I had moved to St. Louis area. This car had several miles on it, so in mid 1965, I traded the Chevy for a new Buick Grand Sport with the 401 engine and a 4 speed. That car was both easy to drive on the street and fun to take to the drag strip. By 1967, the Chevy's and many other muscle cars had become very powerful and the styles were truly phenomenal. This was the muscle car era! What a choice: the GTO's, the GTX's, Road Runners, Camaros, Chevelles, Corvettes, and Ford Mustangs were all amazing.

I then started competing in the sanctioned events at local ¼ mile drag strips; this became a real passion. I enjoy looking back to the muscle car era of the late 60's and early 70's when the cars that are now being restored and are reveling in a resurgence of popularity and values were new and were on the streets of America.

I made my choice and bought a new Chevelle SS 396 convertible in 1967. I drove it on the street but also raced in at the ¼ mile dragstrip. I raced it for a couple of years then blew the engine after changing the cam and adding two four barrel carbs.

In the summer of 1968, I replaced the engine with a 427 cubic inch block from a Corvette, had a well known speed shop rework a set of heads and purchased the latest high performance camshaft. I picked the engine up from the shop and installed it in the Chevelle with the help of some friends. That was a very fast car and I ran competitively in the stock classes with the GTX's and other cars for a year or two. It was at this time I first acquired my nickname of "Fast Eddie" due to my quick reactions reading the lights on the starting line "Christmas tree".

If I was really sharp on a given day, I could come off the line within a fender length of a car I was spotting a light.

Then in 1969, I started dating seriously and was married in 1970. After I was married and had two children, the car fun had to be put on the shelf for many years. I still thought about cars and racing, I enjoyed talking to others and reading car magazines, but I did not have the time or the extra money to spend. Besides, there were so many wonderful experiences to be had while my children were young and I wanted to spend all my time with my family.

It was many years before I got back to cars. After nine years of marriage, my wife and I separated and were divorced. The children went with her and they moved out of state and I went off to Egypt for my two year assignment as a communications consultant, and there was no interest or time to do anything with cars there during those two years.

After completing that assignment, I came back to the U.S. and relocated in the Washington D.C. area on a special assignment. My work assignment there was a special project with a small group of people and the project timeline was very tight. It required many long days with little extra time, except to rest. From there I moved to Atlanta for a second time but did not stay long.

From Atlanta, I moved to Colorado and continued the running but did not do much with cars. However, it was in Colorado where I met and married for the second time. She was an avid runner and enjoyed cars. After two years in Colorado, we moved to Minnesota where my interest in cars was renewed.

I bought a used Porsche and got involved with the Minnesota Nord Stern chapter of the Porsche Club. I started just by talking with the other members and sharing our love of these great performing cars. I then got involved in participating in both low speed and high speed auto cross events. Over a year or so, I made modifications to the car to improve handling performance and also worked to improve my driving skills by participating in multiple events and driving with other clubs.

The Porsche club was a large organization with many great drivers. It was through the autocross events that I met those drivers that also raced at high speed tracks, such as Brainerd International Raceway in Brainerd, Minnesota. This was a whole different ball game; a four mile road course track with a very long, front straight where one mistake at the far turn could send you off the track at a very high speed. Turn two was equally bad. Then, just in case you thought the worst was behind you, there was turn three. It is approximately a 121 degree right hander. In the Porsche I was driving at that time, making that turn properly meant hitting the brakes hard, downshifting from 5th to 3rd and turning hard right.

During the time I was learning this technique, I found a number of new things that I really needed to know: even though you might know how to drive a car fast and you might know how to drive a car with the proper technique, that's not enough. You need to know how to do everything at the same time! Then you need to know how to do all those things when you are in a wheel to wheel race with cars all around you, "nose to tail", and everyone has the same objective of being first.

In my training and practice sessions, I was always working on the technical skills; hitting the apex at each corner just right, and finding the fastest line around the track. I was training my subconscious to make those things automatic. Now rather than having 90 percent of my concentration tied up in those activities, it only took 5 to 10 percent, and then I am able to focus on driving, watching the other cars around me, planning my strategy and thinking of the best spot on that track where I might have an advantage over a particular car and driver. I was able to race in the present moment, with 100 percent concentration.

In the wheel to wheel racing, the driver must really concentrate on the other cars when running in a pack, especially when turning. You quickly find the preferred line around a track, and hitting the ideal apex in each turn becomes very difficult in a race as everyone is basically going for the same spot. If you cannot get the proper line, then you have to be prepared at a split seconds notice to hit the brakes, take a different line, and move over because another car is where you wanted to go.

In a race at Daytona, I was in the middle of a pack of ten cars. We were all within a few inches of each other taking a sharp right hand turn in the infield. This is where the quick reflexes come in; being able to watch the track, attempting to stay on the fastest line through the turn, and being able to watch all the cars around you and adjust quickly as they move one way or the other. At the same time, your car might slip just enough to spin sideways and then you can go careening off the track and into a wall or another car. During that race a car hit a wall very hard in the bus stop area. Parts of the car were scattered all over the track. That session was red flagged and all cars were stopped as soon as possible. I was in that area so I sat in my car for a long time while they removed the driver and cleared the track. The driver was slightly injured but the race was delayed several minutes and we all had to stay in our cars. I was in communication with my crew, including my son who was with me, and I was telling them what was taking place since they couldn't see the backstretch where we were.

I finished both the race and the race weekend without an incident to my car. I did not win my group, however I had issues with my turbo losing boost a couple of times resulting in an extra pit stop which dropped me back in the pack. All in all, it was a great weekend filled with incredible racing, meeting new people and talking with racers from all across the United States. The fact that Daytona is a classic track only added to the competitive spirit and excitement. It was thrilling to know so many of the world class drivers and teams have competed here. It was very special to be there using the actual garages that professional teams use including NASCAR. And to think of the race history at this track is astounding.

One of my most memorable races during the years was racing the Porsche at my home track in Brainerd, Minnesota. Brainerd International Raceway is a very high speed track much like Daytona, even though it does not have the high banking, it is a long track almost four miles long and with a very long front straight followed by a banked turn at the end. Over the years, several cars have gone off the track between the first and second turn. It was a fall weekend and I was running the red Porsche turbo. I had bought it as a street car in good shape, but it had not been set up as a race car. I worked at getting it ready that first summer, and each weekend outing there were issues that needed attention. It required several sessions over a few weekends to get it sorted out. There were times I would not complete a full session of 30 minutes due to an unexpected issue with the car, but when everything was working, it was very fast. I also focused my attention on learning how to drive the car each session so it was faster than my previous session. As I improved, we changed the car setup to fit my driving style, and then we would take another step.

The last weekend at the track fell on a cool fall day and even though the car was running really fast, I felt very comfortable driving it. It fit me like a glove! Saturday afternoon, I was running very close to the track record for our group in that specific class. Each turn felt good, and I felt the car and I were as one.

Sunday was the last track day I had planned to run that year, and it was wet and cool that morning. We all slowed somewhat in the first sessions since the track was cold. After the lunch break, we were all relaxed; the day had been perfect. As we prepared for the afternoon session, someone mentioned that the track was still cooler than normal. I didn't let this bother me because I knew my car set up was good. I felt totally in control, very comfortable and knew I had a chance to break that track's record for my class.

I knew what my time was at every lap; the track timing system was on and was being recorded in the control tower. I also had a timing system in my car. As I ran that first lap, I hit every turn just right by hitting the apex and carrying speed through the turn and squeezing the throttle as early as possible when coming out of the turn. I went into the banked turn at the end of the long front straight with the speedometer somewhere between 155 and 160 miles per hour. Then coming out of turn one, I hit the line for the flat turn two and slowed the car. Then I accelerated through the turn and down the hill to the 121 degree right hand turn three. Turn three was always a challenge as it was very sharp, and in my car I had to brake, downshift from fifth gear to third, then off the brakes and turn in to make the right hander. I was through the turn and on the line for the next turn. I hit the kink just right and the car felt solid. I had turned a car around there in previous races and sessions but had not wrecked. In the first hot lap, as I crossed the start/finish line, I saw I had set a new record. As I sped down the front stretch, I thought great, I did it! Then I patted the dash of my car and said good job. I let off the accelerator for a second and thought I should just enjoy the moment rather than continuing to press hard; then I said to myself, no, we can go faster! Yes, we were working together!

Did you ever have one of those moments when you looked back and said "what was I thinking?" This was one of those. As I went through turn one, I looked toward turn two which was a flat high speed turn. So again, I slowed the car after unwinding from turn one and took the same line as I had on the previous lap. However, I decided to go in about three miles per hour faster than I had the previous lap. I hit the apex just right and squeezed the accelerator down as I came out headed toward turn three. Just as the engine hit full boost and the car was pulling hard, the rear end of the car slid out to the left towards the outside edge of the track. I didn't think this would be bad. I thought I could handle it. I turned the steering wheel to the left to correct the slide and it came back. I was confident it would stick. Unfortunately, within a split second the car went the other way, the rear end slid to the right, I countered to the left, and it came around all the way. I was now sliding sideways nearing the edge of the track. I tried a couple of maneuvers and thought about putting both feet in, which would help stabilize the car. Having the brakes on would slow the car down. However, as I looked to my left to see where I could go, I saw the tree line out at the edge of the grass and was concerned I might hit them. So I attempted to regain control and stay on the track by steering the car back to the middle. The car was beginning to turn back, but I was approaching the inside edge of the track and a dirt bank at a very high speed. I quickly realized that I was not going to save the car, so at the last second I lifted my hands from the wheel and tried to fold them across my chest so I wouldn't break my arms from the impact of the dirt bank. I never did get them folded and the entire time the car was rolling over and over, my arms were bent at the elbows, hands straight up just in front of me. I remember trying to pull them to my chest but I couldn't. The car hit with a thud, my head snapped forward, and I felt the shoulder harnesses pushing into my shoulders and chest as the car flipped up in the air.

Later I heard from the corner worker that was stationed at turn three, that when he turned around to the sound of the impact, my car was standing straight up in the air with the nose about ten feet off the ground. He said he counted five rolls before he realized the car was headed straight for him, so he turned and ran. He said that each time the car hit the ground, great damage was being done and parts were flying from the car. The car finally came to rest on its wheels and as the car hit the ground for the final time, my head hit the "A" pillar by the windshield and I remember it hurting. As I shook my head to see where I was, I saw either smoke or steam rising from the engine. The hood was smashed up in the air and folded back to the windshield. The glass was shattered. As I checked myself, I could not put my feet down on the floor for some reason. I was concerned about the possibility of fire or if I was really hurt, so I looked again at the engine compartment the best I could through the smashed windshield. It was steam I saw, and I did not smell any smoke which was good since my door was jammed shut. Then as I turned to look at my side window, I saw my helmet resting in the grass about 20 feet from the car. I stared in disbelief. If my helmet was out there and I had felt a bump on my head on impact, how badly was I injured. I felt some blood on my head, but it seemed to be ok for the most part.

At this time, the first corner worker came up to the car and pulled the window net down. He asked how I felt. I told him I thought I was ok but had some blood on my head, my left leg hurt and I could not put my feet down on the floor. He reached in and released my shoulder harness. By now there were several workers, emergency crew and paramedics all around the car. I could see at least four already. Someone told me to stay very still and they would get a brace for my neck. Another worker told me they would bring the Jaws of Life tool over because both doors on the car were jammed shut.

As they set the machine in place, someone reached through the window and a second person came in through the other side window. The two of them placed a heavy pad over me so they could remove the car door with Jaws of Life. There was a brief period of lots of noise, and then door was off. The paramedics then brought over a stretcher and began moving me out of the car and onto the board. As I looked around, I could still see my helmet lying in the grass near some seven or eight workers and an emergency crew. They called a good friend of mine that was racing in the event to come out to the scene to be with me. He rode in the ambulance with me to the hospital. As they were lifting me in the back of the ambulance and my friend was climbing in, I looked up at him and said "I got the track record!" The corner workers and emergency crew did a fantastic job taking care of me and handling the incident.

I was wheeled into the hospital and soon after a doctor was examining me. They didn't ask very many questions about what had happened. They were told I was brought in from the race track; plus, I still had pieces of broken glass on my clothes. As it turned out, I was very lucky. I had a bad bruise and cut on the left side of my head, and the doctor said I would have a pretty nasty black eye. I told them my left leg hurt between my knee and hip, so they took a look. There was a small bruise there but no cut and no break. After a few more tests, I was released and my friend and I walked out of the hospital. We then realized that we were brought over in the ambulance, so we had no way back to the track. Thanks to a cell phone, we called a taxi and were back at the track and in the pit area within a few minutes.

My car had been loaded onto a flatbed truck and was parked in the pits where a large crowd was still standing. We got out of the taxi and walked over to my car. The car was totally destroyed. Everyone there welcomed me back and were so glad that I was walking and had no serious injuries. A couple of the corner workers were very shocked. I was very lucky that day and God was undoubtedly with me.

I now had a long ride home and no longer had a race car. My wife was very understanding and was happy that I was not seriously injured. And yes, she did say that I could never race again.

A couple weeks later, she asked me if I was thinking about getting a new car. I said that I would like to but nothing more was said until a month later when she brought it up again. She asked if I was still thinking about getting a car and hesitantly, I said yes. She replied, "Well go get one!"

I located a used Porsche 944 red turbo, like the one before and bought it. It was another street driven car so I had the opportunity to drive it a few times before beginning work to turn it into a race car. While driving it, it didn't feel right. It wasn't comfortable and shortly after, I sold it. Within a few weeks, I bought a black Porsche 944 TS. As soon as I drove it, I knew it was for me. It was perfect.

Over the next few months, I set it up for racing and ran some local events. I finished the car with a full roll cage, reinforced door bars, window and middle restraint netting, radio communications and a cool suit set up. I continued to race this car for three or four years, racing at Daytona with the Porsche Club Racing program and other groups including NASA (National Auto Sports Association) where I ran the Autobahn track in Joliet, IL, as well as running the NASA national event at the Mid Ohio track.

How this affected me and what I learned-

I learned that my involvement and participation in sports over the years was a very positive experience for many reasons. They gave me an outlet for my mind to relax and focus on something other than work or life's problems. They allowed me to meet new people with a common interest outside work and in most cases different people than I met in church or other organizations. I made many good friends and a couple close friends I could go to at anytime. I believe each sport participated in added to my core and gave me new perspectives to later apply to new experiences or challenges.

The friendships made during these times were very special, and when the chips were down, my true friends would know I needed support and would be by my side before I could even ask for help. For example, in 2005 we moved to the Chicago area, and my cancer developed. I did not have the time nor interest of cars so I sold the race car. One of my best friends in the Chicago area knew I was kind of lost and understood that my loss of interest in cars was only temporary. He is a life long car guy, always building and competing with cars. He owns a very successful car restoration business and shares the same love of cars I do. He talked me into getting a classic muscle car and setting it up for street driving and local event competitions. Thanks to him and his persistence, I now own a fun car that I enjoy driving to run errands, participate in autocross events, the ¼ mile drag strip events, and driving on road courses. I really missed and needed that hobby to give me something to do when in need of a boost.

These experiences became a part of my core and were an area that I drew on in several of my life challenges. They helped me cope with situations. I also learned that on the last weekend race in Minnesota when I totaled my car, I should have taken that last turn three miles per hour slower!

Questions for Reflection

1. Do any of the experiences in chapter ten bring back memories for your experiences and what you learned?

2. Have you noticed any benefits from sports or participation in hobbies in your life?

3. Reflect for a moment on how you applied your faith and your life experiences in dealing with a challenge.

4. What book, chapter or verses in the Bible come to mind in reading this chapter?

Chapter Eleven

Moving On

After all my experiences and challenges, where am I today?

I am active with my church small group and am an active Stephen minister. I remain in contact with the American Cancer Society (ACS) and enjoyed being a team captain for the Relay for Life in 2010 and helped others by sharing information. I will always remember the learning experience and support from others in finding my inner core, strength, and faith needed to get through the cancer, treatments, recovery, and dealing with the permanent changes in my life.

I have taken the opportunity to form and lead small groups, and simply be a participant in other groups. I found gems of wisdom and stories of great faith to be inspiring. Learning coping methods from others was a process that made me deeply examine my thoughts and open my mind to discussion. Sharing my personal experiences with others gave me tremendous relief, eased my mind and many times provided new insights for all involved.

Even though I was not one to open up and discuss my issues and deepest feelings initially, through the small groups and the ACS I found this was the exact process I needed to help me through that challenge and prepare me for the next. The support I found within my church and the Stephen Ministry all came together to give me the strength I needed to get through and move on.

This experience confirmed my beliefs in being informed, being in touch with your body, having early and regular testing, and talking openly with your doctor. Those are what I believe to be the primary keys in taking precaution. If I had gone in earlier, my experience with cancer would have been very brief and the treatment would have been much easier. If I had procrastinated a few months longer, the treatments and operation would have certainly been more extensive and in fact, I might not be here today. Today in 2012, I am fortunate to be cancer free for almost four years.

I was lucky with the quick response to my heart attack, as I did not have any long term damage and am capable today of leading an active life. I work outside around the house repairing, building, and digging in the dirt or shoveling snow.

My back problems are minimal. I work out at the club to keep my body strong. I do have to watch how I do certain activities so I do not strain my back. I believe it is important to keep the mind and body strong to be able to do the things you want to do as well as be productive and active. Remember there are seasons of life as there are with the year. There is a time for everything.

I have resumed full time work, regularly exercising at the health club, enjoying my family, walking with my dog and driving my classic car. I benefited from participation in specialized small groups where open, honest discussion and support was stressed. Feeling and hearing the challenges and coping of others was very comforting.

I continue to read and meditate in some form or another, to relax, and exercise to keep my stress level down. Our world seems to be all about keeping busy every moment of the day, always staying in touch with the world by TV, radio, cell phones, or any number of other communication devices and services. It seems we are forgetting how to slow down, be still, and be in touch with ourselves and God.

This past year was the 'Year of the Bible' in our church and many of us read the Bible from cover to cover. I will admit this is the first time I have done this. The readings were everything you might think of: informative, inspirational, baffling, faith building, confusing, scary, and comforting. You need to determine for yourself which ones to read to best comfort or inspire you in your challenge.

One of the verses we read recently in church seemed to be an excellent one to help relax and refocus: "Be still, and know that I am God." (Psalm 46:10 KJV).

Now try reading this slowly and using it as a means to relax, meditate and reflect. Read it again but drop the last word each time you reread it;

Be still, and know that I am God

Be still, and know that I am

Be still, and know I

Be still, and know

Be still

Be

    This simple meditation may seem too easy, or you may think it won't work for you. That is something you will have to try for yourself. You may find that it does not work for you every time, but sometimes it will have a very soothing, calming effect for you.

    I encourage you to use this verse and others that you probably already have, as a means to stop your mind when it is racing, in an unsettled or negative state to bring yourself back to your core and inner peace. The words in this verse do have a very special meaning for me. It brings back wonderful memories of time spent with my paternal grandmother when I was a young boy of only eight or nine.

    I vividly remember walking into the living room of my grandmother's house and finding her in her rocking chair. She was just looking out the window. I asked her what she was looking at; she said I am not looking at anything. I asked her if she was reading even though I did not see a book; she said no, I am not reading. I asked her what she was thinking; she said I am not thinking anything. I probed further as she continued to rock; then what are you doing? She replied, "I am just being."

I have never forgotten this, and now at this stage of my life I believe I can fully understand what my grandmother was saying to me. In our fast paced world, there are many times when I need to go back, remember this, and seek out a space where I can slow down and "just be" for a few minutes. And yes, I do have a real old time rocking chair in my meditation room! Reading this verse while in the rocking chair is very calming for me.

In those extremely difficult times when a person is coping with the death of a loved one, we often talk about the grief we feel and how this triggers such a wide range of feelings and emotions for us. For family members and close friends it may take months or even years to get through the deepest grief and be able to lead a relatively normal life again. For most people, life will never be the same again. We begin to function at a new normal.

Even though we typically associate grief with death, it also can be applied to many other challenges we face. I can tell you from experience that I have felt grief or extreme sadness in more than one of my challenges, knowing that my life would never be the same due to limitation or restrictions placed on me.

I found in those specific medical situations that the more knowledge I had about that situation, (back pain, death, cancer or others) and the more analyzing of my emotions and feelings I did, the better prepared I was to deal with and identify my options. Even though there are pros and cons to assigning labels and time estimates on the emotions and stages in coping, it may be helpful to look at such methods. For example, a search on the internet will provide a listing of the stages of grief (sadness or loss).

The search will not only provide the standard five stages of grief, but also four, seven and ten. Additional searching will produce stages of grief not only for death, but for divorces and unemployment. The typical phases are:

- Denial
- Anger
- Bargaining
- Depression
- Acceptance

In my challenges, I found that it helped me to re-read these descriptions and understand where I was at that time. It helped me realize that even though each day was difficult for me to get through, there were indications that many other people had done so and there was hope that I would eventually accept my new norm of life. I needed to look forward and continue living my life. I did find that although I often identified with the different stages of grief, a schedule could not be put on each stage. Certain stages like anger would surface later even though I knew I had progressed beyond it. I knew in my core and in my heart that if I was still stuck in one of the stages after a year or two, then I was hanging on for some reason rather than moving on.

I knew that I had to grieve but also had to continue on with my life and with those around me. My mind, focus, perception of life and time was being controlled by the challenge I was in. As my list of challenges and experiences grew, I realized I had to cope and move otherwise I may have missed out on what opportunities presented themselves to me. I might have been so wrapped up feeling sorry for myself that I would have missed a great, positive experience.

At some point in each challenge you must come to grips with it and accept the new normal. Life will never be the same as it was and that can't always be looked at as a bad thing. You will find at some point you must find a place to park the feelings and move on, or as Clint Eastwood's character, Walt Kowalski, said to the young guy in the movie Grand Torino, "Man Up". Sorry, I don't know what you ladies would say to that.

And as a friend said to me about my cancer challenge, "Don't waste what you have learned!"

Questions for Reflection

1. Think briefly about a couple of experiences you have had and what your thoughts were afterwards. Did you feel that you learned something or had grown in some respect? If so, how would you describe this?

2. Pick one experience and describe what you have learned.

3. Have you ever gone through any of the stages of grief? If so, do you feel there are absolutely necessary stages to go through when grieving and others you find optional?

4. Was there a time when using a strong emotion such as anger, clenching your teeth and saying "man up" helped get through a tough spot? Is this a method you would frequently rely on or only use in specific situations?

Chapter Twelve

Developing your core support

I did not really begin to develop my core beliefs, faith, support and a true understanding of who I was and what I wanted to do until I was in my mid teens. Thanks to my parents, I started with a deep love and trust in both of them and a profound sense of family. This was combined with a solid faith in God. We talked about God, faith, trust, love and always thinking of others often.

We attended church regularly and were active in Sunday school, church meetings, and in Bible school during the summer. My father was a deacon in the Church at one point as well.

Building upon the foundation I had in my family and church, I began to get an understanding of who I was. I had a sense of belonging and began making decisions about what I wanted to do and become. However it was not until late in high school that I began to truly develop a confidence that allowed me to speak up and express my views, comment on other's ideas, and even disagree at times. That also meant that for the first time I felt confident in spending my time on the friends and activities that I was involved with and really enjoyed. My life became much clearer at that point. I felt comfortable with myself and focused on those activities and events that I enjoyed and wanted to know more about. It was at this time I knew I had a foundation of belief and confidence that I would refer to often and continue to build upon, develop and refine for a long time, probably the rest of my life.

Years later after I was married and had two wonderful children, we were driving on the interstate. My young son and daughter were in the backseat. We were talking about life and how they wished they were older. I commented to them that I had felt the same way when I was very young, but now time had passed very quickly. They asked me to explain that. I simply suggested they visualize the rapid passing of time by turning their heads to look out the side window and focus on how fast the buildings, signs, and utility poles were flashing past as we drove. I said, "That is how fast time goes by."

Here is what the Bible says about time in the book of Ecclesiastes:

A Time for Everything

For everything there is a season,

    A time for every activity under heaven.

A time to be born and time to die.

A time to plant and a time to harvest.

A time to kill and a time to heal.

A time to tear down and a time to build up.

A time to cry and a time to laugh.

A time to grieve and a time to dance.

A time to scatter stones and a time to gather stones.

A time to embrace and a time to turn away.

A time to search and a time to quit searching.

A time to keep and a time to throw away.

A time to tear and a time to mend.

A time to be quiet and a time to speak.

A time to love and a time to hate.

A time for war and a time for peace.

(Ecclesiastes 3:1-9)

The pace of life forces us to delegate more of our time to work and travel than the time we get to spend with our family and friends. We must go forth as the Lord tells us, even though we feel overloaded. The stress level is very high and it leaves little time to truly relax.

We must take initiative and plan our lives so we can take time to relax and enjoy life, meditate, think and just be. For most of us it means finding a way to calm our minds, slow them down and to let go of issues and thoughts that keep our minds spinning.

I read this next excerpt in an article a few years ago and have seen it in various places since. It stresses the importance of letting go and how easy it is for some and how difficult it is for others.

'Two monks were traveling together when they came to a river with a strong current. As the monks were preparing to cross the river, they saw a young woman also attempting to cross. The young woman asked the monks if they could help her.

The younger of the two monks hesitated as they were not supposed to have any physical contact with women. The older monk gently motioned the woman onto his back and proceeded to help the woman across the river. Upon reaching the other bank of the river, the woman got down, thanked the monks and went on her way.

The monks also continued their journey, and it was obvious the younger monk was becoming increasingly agitated and finally spoke out, "Brother, you know we are not permitted to have any contact with women, how could you carry that woman on your shoulders?"

The older monk looked at him and softly replied, "You are right, I did carry that woman. But I have already put her down many hours ago after we crossed the river. Why are you still carrying her?"'

In these situations, many of us still hold strong feelings long after the event. In my experiences with these feelings, I find it to be a huge distraction to my thinking and staying in the present moment when I hang on to things and create stress in my mind and body. Once I realize the cause of my stress, I focus on assessing the feelings. I realize there is no longer any need to retain them, so I release them. I let them go and live in the present moment.

What I have learned and added to my core beliefs has come from many sources. You will have to find what works best for you, and most likely it will be a compilation of a variety of sources. I would recommend two books from John Ortberg, a pastor at Menlo Park Presbyterian Church in California. I have read some of his books and have attended one of the events in which he spoke. In his book, <u>The Me I Want to Be</u>, he speaks about finding out who you are and how there is a person or a "me" you want to be. In another one of his books, <u>If You Want to Walk on Water, You've Got to Get Out of the Boat</u>, he talks about the steps needed in taking an active role in changing your life and moving forward. I benefited from each of them and highly recommend them both.

Questions for Reflection

1. Take a moment to reflect on when your core beliefs (or foundation) began to form. What events have influenced them? Have they ever changed?

2. Thinking of the Ecclesiastes verse in this chapter, pick out a line that is most relevant to your life right now and reflect on the meaning.

3. What methods or processes have you found that help you cope with grief or stress?

4. Thinking about the message in the monks story, reflect on something you need to let go of and identify a first step to take in doing so.

Chapter Thirteen

The Toolbox

I found that during my challenges a gut check of my core beliefs was necessary. As I thought about the emotions I was feeling and the possible coping strategies I could use, I started making a list of words that came to mind that best described what I was feeling. When doing this, I realized that in some situations I had relied more on my religious faith than myself; words I was writing on my list included God, church, Bible, pastoral support, prayers and other similar words. In other challenges, the words and emotions that came to mind were friends, hobbies, sports, joining a group, using humor, meditation and others support, with a lesser reliance on my faith. I then thought of a specific challenge and chose certain words that applied to my thoughts and organized these words in a list or graph which allowed for assessment and reflection. I realized that in a previous challenge I used humor to help me in a tough time but had not used it at all this time. Going through this helped me understand that each challenge and situation is different and what worked last time may not help at all this time. However, by starting with the meanings of a single word and taking a minute to think about what each word meant to me and how the meaning applied or did not apply to the current challenge, helped me to sort out and calm my mind.

Review the following list of words and then take a couple of minutes to reflect on the standard dictionary definitions of each. Then reflect on your own life and experiences to see if your definition or meaning is the same and what emotions or memories might be associated.

After you read through the definition, reflect on how you actually apply that definition in your daily life; see if there is a second or alternate definition that fits your idea or understanding better.

You may find that this brief exercise provides some keen insight to yourself, your true feelings, core beliefs or faith. Perhaps this may spur you to do additional research and might reward you with a self analysis by reading the different meanings or applications of certain words. I suggest you also read the synonyms for each word and think how you currently think of and use those words today.

I have provided one or more definitions and additional information from popular dictionaries in order for you to reflect and assess your core faith and beliefs. They can be used to assist you in dealing with current or future challenges.

Advocate

Definition of Advocate
1. one that defends or maintains a cause or proposal
2. one that supports or promotes the interests of another

Synonyms
supporter, activist, promoter, believer

Believe

Definition of Believe
1. to have a firm religious faith
2. to accept something as true, genuine, or real
3. to have a firm conviction as to the goodness, efficacy, or ability of something
4. to hold an opinion: think

Synonyms
accept, trust, suppose, think

Calling

Definition of Calling
1. a strong inner impulse toward a particular course of action especially when accompanied by conviction of divine influence
2. the particular occupation for which you are trained

Church

Definition of Church
1. a building for public and especially Christian worship
2. the clergy or officialdom of a religious body
3. often capitalized: a body or organization of religious believers:
4. a public divine worship
5. the clerical profession

Synonyms
kirk tabernacle, temple

Confidence

Definition of Confidence
1. a feeling or consciousness of one's powers or of reliance on one's circumstances
2. the feeling or belief that one can rely on someone or something; firm trust
3. the state of feeling certain about the truth of something

Synonyms
self-assurance, self-belief, assurance

Discipline

Definition of Discipline
1. doing what you don't want to do, when you don't want to do it
2. training to act in accordance with rules
3. activity, exercise, or a regimen that develops or improves a skill; training

Synonyms
obedience, regulation, order

Ego

Definition of Ego
1. the self especially as contrasted with another self or the world.
2. the one of the three divisions of psyche in psychoanalytic theory that serves as the organized conscious mediator between the person and reality especially by functioning both in the perception of an adaptation to reality

Synonyms
pride, pridefulness, self-esteem, self-regard, self-respect

Empathy

Definition of Empathy
1. the action of understanding, being aware of, being sensitive to, and vicariously experiencing the feelings, thoughts, and experience of another of either the past or present without having the feelings, thoughts, and experience fully communicated in an objectively explicit manner

Synonyms
compassion, comprehension, understanding, compassion, recognition

Faith

Definition of Faith
1. allegiance to duty or a person : loyalty
2. fidelity to one's promises
3. belief and trust in and loyalty to God
4. belief in the traditional doctrines of a religion
5. firm belief in something for which there is no proof
6. something that is believed especially with strong conviction; especially

The Bible says this in Hebrews 11:1 "Faith is the assurance of things hoped for, the conviction of things not seen."

Synonyms
devotion, piety, religion

Friend

Definition of Friend
1. one attached to another by affection or esteem, acquaintance
2. one that is not hostile
3. one that is of the same nation, party, or group
4. a favored companion

Synonyms
amigo, buddy, chum, compadre, comrade, confidant, confidante, crony, familiar, intimate, mate [chiefly British], musketeer, pal

God

Definition
1. capitalized: a. the supreme or ultimate reality b. the Being perfect in power, wisdom, and goodness who is worshipped as creator and ruler of the universe.

Synonyms
deity, spirit, divinity, all knowing, all powerful, supernatural being.

Grace

Definition of Grace

1. unmerited divine assistance given humans for their regeneration or sanctification 2. a virtue coming from God 3. a state of sanctification enjoyed through divine grace 2. approval, favor

Synonyms
benevolence, boon, courtesy, favor, indulgence, kindness, mercy, service, turn

Grief

Definition of Grief
1. deep and poignant distress caused by or as if by bereavement 2. a cause of such suffering

Synonyms
affliction, anguish, dolefulness, dolor, sorrow, heartache, heartbreak, woe

Heaven

Definition
1. the expanse of space that seems to be over the earth like a dome: firmament —usually used in plural
2. often capitalized : the dwelling place of the Deity and the blessed dead
3. a spiritual state of everlasting communion with God
3. a place or condition of utmost happiness
4. Christian Science: a state of thought in which sin is absent and the harmony of divine Mind is manifest

Synonyms
above, bliss, elysian fields, Elysium, empyrean, kingdom come, New Jerusalem, paradise, sky, Zion, on high

Hell

Definition of Hell
1. a nether world in which the dead continue to exist : hades
2. a: a place or state of misery, torment.
3. a place or state of turmoil or destruction

Synonyms
Gehenna, Pandemonium, perdition, Tophet

Hobby

Definition of Hobby
1. a pursuit outside one's regular occupation engaged in especially for relaxation

Honesty

Definition of Honesty
1. the quality or act of being honest
2. truthfulness, sincerity, or frankness

Synonyms
Integrity, probity, truthfulness, veracity, verity

Hope

Definition of Hope
1. to cherish a desire with anticipation
2. to desire with expectation of obtainment
3. to expect with confidence: trust
4. hope against hope: to hope without any basis for expecting fulfillment

Synonyms
expect, trust, anticipate, expectation, optimism, desire

Humor

Definition of Humor
1. the mental faculty of discovering, expressing, or appreciating the ludicrous or absurdly incongruous
2. something that is or is designed to be comical or amusing

Synonyms
comedy, , drollery, funniness, hilariousness, humorousness,

Inspiration

Definition of Inspiration
1. a divine influence or action on a person believed to qualify him or her to receive and communicate sacred revelation
2. the action or power of moving the intellect or emotions
3. the act of influencing or suggesting opinions

Love

Definition of Love
1. strong affection for another arising out of kinship or personal ties
2. warm attachment, enthusiasm, or devotion
3. unselfish loyal and benevolent concern for the good of another

Synonyms
affection, attachment, devotedness, devotion, fondness, passion

Loyalty

Definition of Loyalty
1. strong feeling of support of allegiance
2. a feeling or attitude of devoted attachment and affection

Synonyms
allegiance, attachment, devotion, obedience, steadfastness, sincerity

Meditation

Definition of Meditation
1. the act or process of meditating
2. a devotional exercise of or leading to contemplation
3. meditation is a practice of concentrated focus upon a sound, object, visualization, the breath, movement, or attention itself in order to increase awareness of the present moment, reduce stress, promote relaxation, and enhance personal and spiritual growth

Synonyms
concentration, deep thought, introspection, pondering, quiet time, reflection, rumination, self-examination

Mindfulness

Definition of Mindfulness
1. the trait of staying aware of (paying close attention to) your responsibilities
2. cautious attentiveness

Synonyms
heedfulness, regard, care, carefulness, caution

Mission

Definition of Mission
1. a ministry commissioned by a religious organization to propagate its faith or carry on humanitarian work
2. a specific task with which a person or a group is charged

Synonyms
assignment, charge, operation

Participate

Definition of Participate
1. to take part in
2. to have a part of share in something

Synonyms
Partake, share

Passion

Definition of Passion
1. often capitalized a: the suffering of Christ between the night of the Last Supper and his death
2. the state of capacity of being acted on by external agents or forces
3. emotions as distinguished from reason b: intense, driving, or overmastering feeling or conviction
4. ardent affection: love
5. strong liking or desire for or devotion to some activity, object, or concept
6. an object of desire or deep interest

Synonyms
affection, attachment, devotedness, devotion, fondness, love.

Prayer

Definition of Prayer
1. pleading, especially with a deity
2. a solemn request for help or expression of thanks addressed to God or an object of worship

Synonyms
plea, begging, benediction, request, desire, hope

Purpose

Definition of Purpose
1. The reason for which something is done or created or for which something exists
2. an intended or desired result, end, aim, goal
3. determination; resoluteness
4. the subject in hand; the point at issue

Synonyms
intention, mean, reason, rationale

Respect

Definition of Respect
1. a relation or reference to a particular thing or situation
2. an act of giving particular attention : consideration
3. high or special regard: esteem

Synonyms
reference, regard

Support

Definition of Support
1. to endure bravely or quietly
2. to promote the interests or cause of
3. to uphold or defend as valid or right

Synonyms
Sustain, favor, uphold, help

Support Group

Definition of Support Group
1. a group of people, sometimes led by a therapist, who provide each other moral support, information, and advice on problems relating to some shared characteristic or experience

---

Example matrices and graphs are included here to use as a means of self assessment and reflection. Use the words listed above to fill in the organizational charts. I suggest picking at least two different situations or challenges you have dealt with in the past; write down words under the appropriate headings that describe the coping methods you used during those times. You may choose to use additional words that I have not included. You may need to experiment with different charts or formats before finding what makes most sense to you. Once your graph is completed, take a moment to reflect on whether you relied more on faith and religion or self and community.

There is no right or wrong way to fill out a chart or deal with a situation. This is not a professional assessment but rather an exercise meant for introspection. You will be able to see what skills you are using and not using, and see if you think those skills worked for you in the particular situation. You may find what you have done in the past has worked for you, or you may find that you are at a point where you need additional support from a support group or professional. Never hesitate to seek professional help.

In the first example, I placed words from the toolbox definitions either in the category of religion or self. Those words represent emotions I felt or actions I took when coping. In looking at this example, I am able to see I relied more on religion than I did myself to cope with this particular situation.

Religion

God
Faith
Prayer
Church

Belief   Honesty
Christian   Hope
Group   Humor
Bible   Love
                        Self

I reflected on a different situation below, and I can see I relied more on myself than I did on religion in this particular situation. In retrospect, if I were in this same situation again, I would have placed more reliance in God and my faith than self.

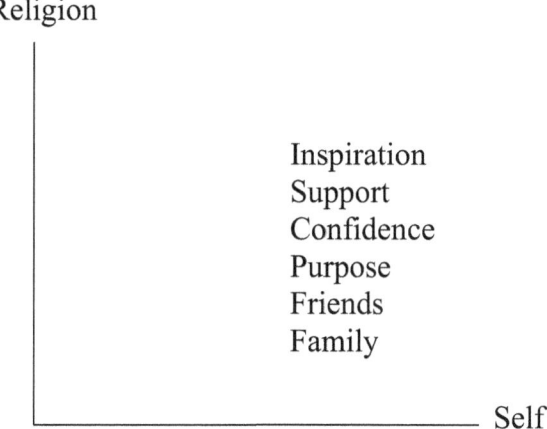

The second example uses two columns rather than a graph:

Religion	Self or Community
God	Ego
Church	Hobbies
Bible	Sports
	Reading

The purpose in going back and using the graphs or charts to plot the words is to see what works for you as an individual. I have found that a few things have consistently worked for me in each challenge to help me relax, de-stress, relieve tension and remain engaged in life rather than withdrawing and dwelling on my situation. They are basic things to use anytime to slow down, and calm the body and mind.

- Be in or think about pleasant scenery
- Think of good memories
- Relax your body
- Concentrate on your breathing; breathe in through your nose and slowly breathe out through your mouth
- As you concentrate on your breathing, do not let negative thoughts enter your mind
- Try counting or repeating a relaxing verse of thought
- Drink plenty of water, stay well hydrated
- Get a massage
- Meditate or practice yoga
- Spend 15 to 20 minutes in a rocking chair
- Avoid angry people or watching or listening to unpleasant news
- Think positive thoughts
- Rely on others; there really are a lot of people out there willing to help you
- Read to self, read to others, read to a pet
- Listen to soothing music and sounds
- Work out
- Go for a walk or run outside- see God's world
- Go on a bike ride through a park

You may find that time moves too fast or too slow during times of stress. I often use the term time perception or control rather than time management. My intent is to have you think in terms of your perception of the passing of time, not necessarily what you are doing in a specific time period or how efficiently you are working. Time control is about how you can slow time down during the good times and speed it up during others, or at least rewire your mind to better deal with a period of time and how you perceive the passing of time.

As an example, think of when you were in school and the school week seemed so long, yet Spring Break seemed to go by so very fast.

Another example would be if you are working out and have a program mapped out to improve x% in a specific amount of time. The first few weeks may seem as if time is passing slowly, perhaps even painfully slow. Then as you progress, it may seem that time passes very quickly and your goal was met sooner than anticipated.

A situation in which time seems to move slowly is when you are healing from an injury. The weeks of healing seem to last forever and this is a time where you would want time to pass quickly.

If you want to slow time down, read a book, or sit and just be. Time will seem to pass at a much slower rate. I find I need to remember to apply time perception control when I am stressed. Most often it is when I feel time is passing too fast and I am falling behind, late for appointments or always rushing to get something done. That creates stress and robs me of my core strength. You may find your mind is thinking negative thoughts. In that case, you must tell yourself to stop! I would recommend research on time perception. One excellent book is <u>Time Shifting: Creating More Time to Enjoy Your Life</u> by Stephan Rechtschaffen.

Questions for Reflection

1. What is your general perception of time during the work week? During the weekends or your time off?

2. Are there times in your life when you would like time to speed up or slow down?

3. Do you have a quiet place to go to meditate or just clear your mind and calm yourself?

4. Do you have a phrase, a favorite Bible verse or a saying to calm yourself when time is passing too fast or you are stressed?

Chapter Fourteen

Be an Advocate

In today's world of fast paced conversation and exchange of information, it seems everyone is in fast forward. No one has time to really talk and ask questions, receive thoughtful answers, or have an honest and insightful sharing of information that allows for a genuine connection. We all are in such a hurry we contact someone by phone, text or email just to give them our own information. We seem to have lost the art of asking questions to really draw out true thoughts from the other person, or attempt to understand why someone is reaching out to us to share a concern or ask for help. What has happened to a good two sided conversation?

Most of us need to take the time to understand where we are, what we're feeling, and what information we need in order to make solid, informed decisions. We should be our own advocate. When we meet with someone; ask questions, ask why and ask what the options are.

When you talk with your doctor, ask follow up questions. Don't let them give you the "two minute" brush off, then they are out the door and on to the next patient before you have even processed the information. Be your own advocate!

Take initiative; it's your life. There are other doctors available and you may find that a different doctor will be a better fit for your needs, experience or comfort level with the particular individual. It may depend more on their communication style or personality. In some cases, just the way the office staff and medical assistants or nurses associated with the practice may make the difference between dreading a visit to the doctor, or having a comfortable experience. I think that some of us certainly experience some level of apprehension when we have to visit the doctor's office, dentist office, other medical specialists or the hospital. It may help to question the things in our control and address any changes that might reduce some of the possible stress associated with these visits.

Sometimes it may be best to prepare questions and concerns prior to to your appointment, then call ahead and talk to someone in the office or other medical professional. I have prepared a written list of questions and handed the list to my doctor as soon as he walked in. I have also left the doctor's office, then turned around and walked right back in to ask a question. I often request a copy of any tests or reports so I can review them, compile my thoughts and have them on file for future reference.

I believe being an advocate starts with a person truly being involved in life, listening, actively participating and interacting with others in all walks and activities of life. It means genuinely being interested in life and in others that we live with, our friends, the people we work with, our church members and those we meet each day. I believe you can meet someone and get to know them in a very brief time, at least to the level that you have a gut feeling about them based on the sharing of ideals, thoughts, goals and beliefs. If you have an honest exchange with someone and find some common ground, if you open up and let yourself connect with that person, you will feel a desire to be an advocate for them in moving forward, solving a problem, or in praying for them. Be an advocate for them or perhaps you can help them become their own advocate.

I added a new area to my core faith and strength a year after my bout with cancer in 2008. The whole experience starting with the diagnosis in the spring of 2008 continuing through the tests, chemotherapy, radiation treatments, my operation, the healing and recovery process, really took a toll on me both physically and mentally. I was in a fog mentally and this shook my core. I was not as positive or confident for many months as I had previously been.

During the whole process, I had the feeling this was for a reason; that this was one of those lessons I needed to learn, or an experience that was given to me by God so that I would be prepared for an event soon to come into my life.

During the recovery period, I began searching for a mission or cause that I should be a part of. After much inner searching, I knew that it would involve increasing my compassion and in finding the best place that I could provide some level of support and care for others who needed it. I found that mission through my church, in the form of Stephen Ministries.

I signed up for the very next training program and began my training. The Stephen Ministries organization is a non-profit, transdenominational, religious and educational organization. It trains and organizes lay people to provide one-to-one Christian care to those who need it in the area. It was one of the best decisions I have made and has been enlightening for me. The instructors were very knowledgeable and had provided support to care receivers. The excellent training, the application of their training and experience, combined with the role playing in class was extremely effective. I knew that I was already looking forward to being a caregiver even though I was very apprehensive when signing up for the class. I completed the training and was commissioned as a Stephen Minister in 2009.

Since that time, I have completed assignments as a caregiver through the program as well as providing caring support to a neighbor couple in their last months before passing away.

The program is very strong with an excellent formal training program and ongoing supervision meetings that support the caregivers and provides guidance in the care giving process. I have also found that it truly helped me as a person in my everyday life to be more understanding of others and of myself. I found that the training, the experiences and the association with other Stephen Ministers gave me added strength and comfort in my core support.

I continue to be an avid reader and among the authors that I read, John Ortberg is one that I read frequently. He has written a number of books and I particularly like a couple of them and have co-hosted small group sessions discussing two of the books; <u>Everybody's Normal Till You Get to Know Them</u> and <u>If You Want to Walk on Water, You've Got to Get Out of the Boat</u>.

The one I am thinking of is one of his latest, <u>The Me I Want to Be: God's Best Version of You</u>. In this book, Ortberg gets the reader to think and reflect in order to gain an accurate self perception and be able to identify an area of need to focus on.

One quote from Ortberg's <u>The Me I Want to Be</u> is borrowed from accredited author John Milton who said, "The mind is its own place, and can make a heaven of hell, or a hell of heaven."

I will remind you in closing this chapter that you can certainly be a self-advocate. You definitely should question areas where someone is providing a professional service to you or any other service where you are the consumer paying money to someone else for services or products. You should have the right to check and question the end result and fees. Do not hesitate to question anything you do not understand.

I encourage you to write a letter to a company or office providing a service or product that you have an issue with. I developed a form that I call a "Notice of Unacceptable Action" that I have completed and sent to an office or company where I have received less than satisfactory service. It is very simple and straightforward in stating the specific area of disappointment. It has been very effective for me, and I felt better for doing it. I found that it allowed me to vent my frustration and move on. (You can make your own form or outline and at the end of the letter or form be certain to list a cc of "everybody!")

Questions for Reflection

1. Do you consider yourself an advocate? Are you your own advocate?

2. Are you currently an advocate for anyone or any cause? Briefly note or discuss what the cause is and how it has impacted your life.

3. Think about different ways you could be an advocate for or provide support for someone, or for a cause.

4. Discuss how you think Christian care might be different from other care giving.

Chapter Fifteen

Your Mission

You probably have had a mission in your life at one time or another that you were fully aware of and set goals to fulfill it. On the contrary, there may have been times when you were not fully aware of the mission you were on. You may have been given the opportunity to get involved in a project with your church, community or an organization yet you did not see the bigger picture in the beginning. Perhaps it wasn't until careful reflection that you realized the purpose for your circumstances and the mission you were on. Maybe you have a great mission in mind but that opportunity has not yet presented itself. This may be a time to concentrate on what opportunities you may have had and, or have now and just are too busy to see what is being offered to you. Many times we are so busy that we miss the excellent opportunities that are in front of us.

I believe we each have one or more individual missions in our lives. Perhaps we have already served in a special capacity to someone and were not even aware of what support or caring we were providing to someone in need.

If you reflect on your life, you might identify a unique time period when it just seemed the time was right you do something for someone, or help a stranger. It may or may not have been accompanied by a bolt of lightning or divine guidance. It may have been a goal that you were working toward that benefited someone else.

One of the books I like about goals or having a plan is <u>Game Plan for Life</u> by Joe Gibbs. This is a great book that's enjoyable to read and presents a perspective that emphasizes how important it is to have a game plan in life. Joe Gibbs has been very successful with many major accomplishments including winning three Super Bowl titles as the Head coach of a professional football team and winning NASCAR professional racing championships as a team owner.

Although I have never played football, I have raced cars on many tracks including Daytona. Having a plan for the race wasn't the only critical part, but there's also a time element as to the time or distance of the race and the way the driver handles the time during the race. Although there are many ways you can dissect this element, I am referring to the phenomena of how a focus, mindfulness, or how the driver sees time second by second can change the perception of time. They can slow time down so everything almost seems in slow motion. We have read or heard of running backs talking about getting in the "zone" or specific mental state during the run of a big game where everything seems to be in slow motion and they can just run around the tacklers. I have experienced this timeshifting in both running races as well as in car racing.

During the time my wife and I lived in Minnesota, I heard about a book on timeshifting and the approach described by Dr. Stephan Rechtschaffen M.D.

I found a seminar and workshop being held in Minneapolis that allowed a few people to participate in the experience of timeshifting. I signed up and attended the one day seminar. What an experience; this made a believer of me!

The session started with us checking in, in an office environment, then being asked to take off our watches and hand over our cell phones. There was a small group of some 15 people and we were ushered into an interior room without any windows, clocks or any time telling device. We were then informed that during our time in the room, we would do or not do certain things so that our perception of time would be altered. For example, we were told the seminar would be completed by the end of the day, but it could be anytime between early afternoon and sundown. We would have at least one break and would be served a lunch in that room, but it may or may not be served at a typical lunchtime.

The principle of timeshifting became clear to me after a raisin exercise. In this exercise, we were all seated and were each given a raisin to hold in our hand. We were then instructed to close our eyes and keep them closed during this exercise. The leader instructed us in a low, calm voice, to feel the raisin's texture and size, and then place the raisin in our mouth very gently. We were told to close our mouth and hold the raisin on our tongue, clearing our mind of any thoughts other than our concentration on the raisin. We were instructed to roll the raisin around and feel and taste the sweetness while visualizing it.

After what seemed like a few minutes, but could have been a half hour, we were allowed to swallow it.

It was amazing how good that raisin tasted and how satisfying it was. That really brought home the experiences awaiting us as we slowed time down. That was probably one of the first times I had concentrated on being in the present moment and being mindful for that long. Later on when I was racing cars, I used this experience to stay in the present moment the entire duration of the race.

Planning your life

There are those truly gifted people in the world that just seem to know what their life is about, where their focus should be, what their purpose is, and exactly where they are in that plan. Some people seem to have known this plan early on in life while many others are not that fortunate or focused. We may have ideas of who we are, what we want to do, and who we eventually want to be.

Then there are those that do not have a road map or life plan, and they are content to live day by day. It is easy to get sidetracked or wait for a really special opportunity.

I remember someone saying to me many years ago, "I awake each day torn between changing the world or enjoying the world."

I believe we all need time to enjoy the world and a day off is needed sometimes to rest and reflect. I think we are truly happiest when we are focused on something. Anytime we are involved in a cause it seems to increase our awareness and interest in those around us.

I like the way Dr. Porsche of the Porsche automobile family put it;

> "Life itself is a race, marked by a start, and a finish. It is what we learn during the race, and how we apply it, that determines whether our participation has had particular value. If we learn from each success, and each failure, and improve ourselves through this process, then, at the end, we will have fulfilled our potential and performed well."

In one of my long time favorite books, <u>The Power of Positive Thinking</u> by Norman Vincent Peale, there are many pages of excellent advice and techniques for clearing your mind and allowing positive thoughts to come in. Then applying that positive mind set to stay on focus and share the positive outlook in your conversations, your actions and your life. It will influence other's lives and will also come back to you as a positive force. In other words, give and it will come back to you.

One of the techniques used in the book is that of practicing the daily habit of silence. He recommends that everyone should spend at least a quarter of an hour in absolute silence every twenty four hours. Find a quiet spot to clear your mind, then began to listen for the deeper harmony that can be found in the silence. In my experience, I have found it is in these times that the new, clean, positive thoughts come into my mind and provide a calm and peace that generates new power, peacefulness and ideas.

Perhaps we all have this mission in us, just waiting for us to make the extra effort. Maybe we just need a nudge or reminder every so often to get us motivated and keep us moving forward.

I have five books I keep within my reach and refer to often. They may not all be for you but I highly recommend you check them out (at least the first one):

- The Bible

- <u>The Power of Positive Thinking</u> by Norman Vincent Peale.

- <u>Game Plan for Life</u> by Joe Gibbs.

- <u>Time Shifting</u> by Stephan Rechtschaffen M.D.
- <u>The Me I Want to Be</u> by John Ortberg.

Questions for Reflection

1. Are you currently involved in a cause, mission or calling?

2. If you are, reflect on what you are doing and how your life is different now because of this mission.

3. If you are not, reflect back on a previous mission.

4. If you are interested in a new future mission, list at least two special areas that you are interested in and how to begin getting involved.

Chapter Sixteen

What does it all mean?

At this point, you should be feeling open and receptive to new thoughts and ideas, but most importantly you should be at a point that you can be honest with yourself.

Before we can feel like we have a purpose or perhaps an overarching goal in life, we have to ask ourselves if we really believe deep in our core being that we can commit to a mission or purpose.

When reflecting on my life, I have found that not only is the present moment crucial to consider but also to be mindful of my entire life and the generations that preceded me that impact who I am.

A quick example; I came across a post card a couple of years ago that was written to my grandfather in 1909 mailed to him by a friend. My son was named after my grandfather and in the fall of 2009, I sent this postcard to my son for his birthday. To me, that is a very special connection that spans 100 years. It reminds me of the special bond and love between family.

Being committed to a purpose means that we are so comfortable with our mission that we are thinking about it often, telling our family, friends, neighbors and perhaps even casual acquaintances.

We get to that point by believing in our core faith and knowing that the mission or goal we have stated is attainable in our mind and heart. If it is, we will find that we will be focused and find ways to accomplish it. I have personally experienced this in different ways; from my running background, to racing cars, to different jobs I have had, to accepting the overseas assignment against all advice, to other personal challenges such as the cancer experience and in setting and reaching specific goals. Some were short term, and others were quite long.

I believe this truly happens when you use all your capabilities to think this through in your mind, to feel it in your heart, to verify it through your conscious and subconscious mind and set the goal. Write it down and check to see that it is possible. Then take a look at the goal or mission from your core. Do you really believe you will actually do this and that *you*, not talking about anybody else, are willing to work towards it.

For instance, if you set a goal to earn $1,000,000 in the next 12 months does that seem realistic? If you think no, you are setting yourself up to fail. However, if during this process you really and truly believe that you could earn an extra $10,000 in the next 12 months, then that might be a better approach for you, as your entire being will focus on your mission. It's realistic. Be real, be committed, be diligent, and believe!

Remember, this is about you as an individual and what works for one person may not work for the next. Some people need to set their goals very high and it's ok if they don't quite reach them. They just set a new goal once they have attained a certain level of success and move on. There is nothing wrong in setting a series of steps toward your goal.

The key point I found was having a goal that I really believed I could reach. When I had it in my mind, I would actually find times when I was able to relax and let my subconscious mind take over in working towards my mission.

I have found that by having a positive attitude and an open, hopeful outlook on life, I have something to look forward to each day. That in itself gives each new day a purpose and a reason to get up. You may need to remind yourself on occasion, that there may be days when it seems there is nothing special or meaningful for you, and that will certainly happen. However, keep in mind that on those days, it may be you doing something that really helps someone else, or brightens their day. So it is not always about you; you are alive that day, at that time and in a specific place because God has a purpose for you.

There will be different perspectives regarding this area depending on your personal view, your faith, and what each of us would define or consider a mission. Many believe a mission is a major task or charge in life given by God. Others may believe that it comes from some other higher power or force; while others may simply believe it comes from us and our own thoughts. Whatever you believe, I hope you have, or will find your mission. If we were to really stop and assess what we are currently involved in and assess our individual strengths and weaknesses, we might find that we are in fact perfectly suited to do what we are currently doing whether it be our job, career, an activity we are doing, outside work with a volunteer group, an organization or religious group.

I believe I was on a mission to write this book as I had never had any aspirations to be an author and did not feel I had a story to tell. However, I did get the inspiration for this book in a dream the night of September 4th, 2010, and the title of the book and the titles of six chapters were in my mind the next morning when I awoke. September 4th was my son's birthday.

In my dream that night of September 4th, someone walked up to me and handed me a book, a book with a dark blue or black cover. As I reached out to take the book, I could read the plain cover that simply said 'I Believe, by Ed Hazelwood'.

Upon waking, I went downstairs and made a pot of coffee. I sat at my computer and started the book. I created the cover page, listed six chapter titles, then started writing chapter one.

From September 5th until early November, I would wake up with new words and thoughts in mind that I wanted in the book. I was writing and providing more details almost on a daily basis. In early to mid November, my writing began to taper off and I was then thinking and observing more in my waking hours. I listened more closely to every conversation and found sometimes the conversation would later trigger new thoughts for the book. At this time, I was really thinking about the emotions and words I had used and how they had meaning to me and in many cases could be looked at as tools that were different from experience to experience. They were in a sense the tools I used to cope with different experiences.

I continued to expand that list. In some cases, I replaced some words with others. I then spent some time refining the list and starting to lay out some sort of means of analysis and self evaluation that would be helpful to me and hopefully to you in assessing and developing coping strategies.

Then from late November to the end of December, I didn't really have inspired words and did not spend much time writing new material. In mid December, I did start having visual dreams almost each night and began attempting to recall the dream or dreams first thing in the morning. As they continued, I decided there must be a reason for this so I began to record each night's dreams in a dream journal. I found that I had at least one dream I could recall each morning, and some nights I had as many as three. That continued until January 6th and then stopped for a few nights with no dreams being recalled. I started dreaming again later and had several significant dreams over the next few months.

Humor and Laughter

I have found that humor and bouts of real, heartfelt, good out loud laughter relieves stress and makes me feel better.

For a more technical description, read what NASA (National Aeronautics and Space Administration) says in a Health Bulletin, Number 51, from a few years ago entitled <u>Rx Laughter</u>:

<u>The Healing Gift.</u>

Signs and Symptoms: Due to the involuntary simultaneous contraction of 15 facial muscles, the upper lip is raised, partially uncovering the teeth and affecting a downward curving of the furrows that extend form the wings of both nostrils to the corners of the mouth. This produces a puffing out of the cheeks on the outer side of the furrows. Creases also occur under the eyes and may become permanent at the side edges of the eye. The eyes undergo reflex lacrimation and vascular engorgement. At the same time, an abrupt strong expiration of air is followed by spasmodic contractions of the chest and diaphragm resulting in a series of expiration- inspiration microcycles with interval pauses. The whole body may be thrown backward, shaken or convulsed due to other spasmodic skeletal muscles contractions.

Diagnosis: Belly-laughter.

Prognosis: Improved sense of health and well-being.

Of all human expressive behaviors, laughter has proved a most fascinating enigma to philosophers and scientists alike. Its physiology, neurology and anthropological origins and purposes are only partially defined. But its effects and uses are becoming increasingly apparent to health care professionals.

Laughter is considered to be an innate human response which develops during the first few weeks of life. Evidence of the innate quality of laughter is seen in its occurrence in deaf and blind infants and children who are completely without visual or auditory cues from their social environment. Darwin propounded in his "Principle of Antithesis" that laughter developed as the infant's powerful reward signal of comfort and well-being to the nurturing adult. This signal is totally antithetical perceptually to the screams or cries of distress associated with discomfort. Laughter seems to play an important role in the promotion of social unity, production of a sense of well-being, communication of well-being, and as a mechanism for coping with stressful situations. Physiologically, both reflexive (tickle-response) and "heart-felt" (mental-response) laughter affect changes to the human system which may be significant in the treatment and prevention of illness. These include laughter's association with:

-an increase in pulse rate, probably due to increased levels of circulatory catecholamines (Blood catecholamine levels vary directly with the intensity of laughter.)

-an increase in respiration

- a decrease in blood-CO_2 levels

- a possible increase in secretion of brain and pituitary endorphins- the body's natural anesthetics which relieve pain, inhibit emotional response to pain, and thus reduce suffering

- a decrease in red blood cell sedimentation rate ("Sed rate" is associated with the body's level of infection or inflammation.)

Perspective on Laughter

Immanuel Kant, in his Critique of Pure Reason, wrote: "Laughter produces a feeling of health through the affection that moves the intestines and the diaphragms; in a word, the feeling of health that makes up the gratification felt by us; so that we can thus reach the body through the soul and use the latter as the physician of the former." Echoing Kant's thesis nearly two centuries later, Norman Cousins, author, senior lecturer at the UCLA School of Medicine, and editor of *Saturday Review* has become the modern day patron saint of self-potentiation through the healing power of laughter. Recognizing the effects of "Negative emotions" upon body chemistry, health, and well-being, Cousins questioned whether positive emotions such as love, hope, faith, confidence, and laughter might have positive therapeutic value.

We are all in this life for a number of years, hopefully several. It is a great and wonderful journey from the experiences we have as children; so secure in the knowledge, warmth and love of our parents, the laughter and play with our childhood friends, the knowledge and great experiences we avail ourselves of and become wiser from to us as adults, to mentor others and serve as a guide and role model.

Think about how exciting it is to learn about the world we live in, the absolute grandness and awe inspiring natural beauty of our Earth and heavens, the vast amount of discovery and mass of knowledge accumulated by those that preceded us. We have the opportunity to learn from what others have done, build on that, press forward to higher levels of knowledge and even greater discoveries, greater advancements and new inventions.

I believe we should have, and need a game plan for our life and definitive mission that we believe in with all our heart and soul. A different way to look at it is that God gave each one of us a talent or gift to use. Do you know what your gift is and are you using it?

Always have an open, listening mind; there are many new needs and ideas out there. By listening and being receptive you are preparing yourself for a new challenge or opportunity. You could be the one to help that person in need, to bring forth that new idea or service to benefit many.

My wife will sometimes say to me as we are getting ready to go out, "Are you going out like that?" Perhaps not only should we check what we are wearing, but also check the state our mind is in. Is your head right before you go out in a hurry and drive in heavy traffic or talk with others about the state of the economy, religion or politics? If you are having a bad day and your attitude is negative, that will influence your reaction to those you meet during the day. How about stopping for a moment before you open the door and checking your attitude. Work on having a positive attitude, stay in the present moment and "give more, to get more."

Questions for Reflection

1. Do you believe you have been given a talent or gift from God? If so, what?

2. Are you using this talent? If not, do you have plans?

3. What or who inspires you?

4. Are you comfortable with your ego, core, faith and who you are? If not, what would you change?

Reader Notes:

Reader notes cont.

Reader notes cont.

Reader Notes cont.

Thoughts for meditation and in finding peace of mind:

- What is, is, what is not, is not. So be it! (Dr. Indra K. Somani).

- Be kind to others, they may not know your expectations of them.

- As long as you are breathing there is more right with you than there is wrong. (Ohm Johari, Phd)

- Try to live to be the person your dog thinks you are (Ed)

Watch for other books from Ed –

The Dax Adventure Series (Children's books)

Old Time sayings and Advice from Missouri

The End

www.ingramcontent.com/pod-product-compliance
Lightning Source LLC
Chambersburg PA
CBHW061431040426
42450CB00007B/1003